THE UNITED STATES AT WAR

THE WAR OF 1812

Karen Clemens Warrick

Enslow Publishing
101 W. 23rd Street
Suite 240
New York, NY 10011
USA

enslow.com

Published in 2017 by Enslow Publishing, LLC.
101 W. 23rd Street, Suite 240, New York, NY 10011

Library of Congress Cataloging-in-Publication Data
Names: Warrick, Karen Clemens.
Title: The War of 1812 / Karen Clemens Warrick.
Description: New York, NY : Enslow Publishing, 2017. | Includes bibliographical references and index.
Identifiers: LCCN 2016005256 | ISBN 9780766076716 (library bound)
Subjects: LCSH: United States—History—War of 1812—Juvenile literature.
Classification: LCC E354 .W38 2017 | DDC 973.5/2—dc23
LC record available at http://lccn.loc.gov/2016005256

Printed in the United States of America

To Our Readers: We have done our best to make sure all websites in this book were active and appropriate when we went to press. However, the author and the publisher have no control over and assume no liability for the material available on those websites or on any websites they may link to. Any comments or suggestions can be sent by e-mail to customerservice@enslow.com.

Portions of this book appeared in the book *The War of 1812: "We Have Met the Enemy and They Are Ours."*

Photo Credits: Series logo on cover and p. 1 Memory Stockphoto/Shutterstock.com (insignia), Sergey Kamshylin/Shutterstock.com (US flag); cover, pp. 1, 6 UniverallmagesGroup/Getty Images; pp. 4–5 Everett Historical/Shutterstock.com; pp. 18, 22, 38, 44, 92, 102 Library of Congress, Prints and Photographs Division; p. 9 Jose Gil/Shutterstock.com; p. 14 New York Public Library, USA/Bridgeman Images; p. 17 Library of Congress/Mary Evans; p. 20 Fine Art Images/ Heritage Images/Hulton Archives/Getty Images; pp. 25, 30, 64 © North Wind Picture Archives; pp. 36, 74 Private Collection/Ken Welsh/Bridgeman Images; pp. 42, 62 Kean Collection/Hulton Archive/Getty Images; p. 50 Superstock; p. 54 File: U.S.S. Constution1803/Wikipedia Commons; p. 57 Popperfoto/Getty Images; p. 73 Fuse/Thinkstock; pp. 78, 90, 120 MPI/ Archive Photos/Getty Images; p. 81 © GeoStills/Alamy Stock Photo; p. 84 Photo by Lombard/ullstein bild via Getty Images; p. 101 © Gerry Embleton/North Wind Picture Archives; p. 106 © Collection of the New York Historical Society, USA/Bridgeman Images; pp. 108, 118 De Agostini Picture Library/Bridgeman Images; p. 127 © AP Images; p. 128 Stock Montage/ Archive Photos/Getty Images; p. 130 © Mcs2 Peter Melkus Planet Pix via ZUMA Wire/ZUMA Press; p. 132 Joyce Naltchayan/AFP/Getty Images.

CONTENTS

FOREWORD

By the summer of 1814, Baltimore, Maryland, expected the British Royal Navy to attack. Major George Armistead, the commander at Fort McHenry, had spent months preparing to defend the city. All the fortifications were in place, but there was one item missing. Major Armistead desired "to have a flag so large that the British will have no difficulty seeing it from a distance." He got his wish.

Two flags were ordered from Mary Pickersgill. She was Baltimore's best known flag maker. Mary and her thirteen-year-old daughter, Caroline, worked tirelessly on the projects. One flag, called a "storm flag" measured 17 feet by 25 feet (5 m x 7.6 m).

The second flag was to be the largest ever flown over a fort. It measured 30 feet by 42 feet (9 m x 13 m). Each stripe was 2 feet (.6 m) wide and the stars were 24 inches (60 cm) from point to point. In 1814, the United States Flag had 15 stars and 15 stripes. At that time one star and stripe were added for each new state that joined the union. The thirteen original colonies and new states of Kentucky and Vermont were represented on the 1814 flag.

Both flags were completed before the British sailed up the Chesapeake to attack Fort McHenry on September 13, 1814. The next morning, following a night of relentless British bombardment, Pickersgill's flag waved proudly over the star-shaped ramparts of Fort McHenry. The sight inspired Francis Scott Key who had been detained overnight on a British ship. He began a poem to commemorate the occasion. It was first published under the title "Defense of Fort M'Henry." The poem soon attained wide popularity and was sung to the tune "To Anacreon in Heaven." In 1931, this song, now known as "The Star-Spangled Banner," was officially made the National Anthem by Congress.

Today the famous Fort McHenry flag is displayed in the Smithsonian Institution's National Museum of American History, in Washington, D.C. The storm flag is lost to history.[1]

The Star-Spangled Banner

O say, can you see, by the dawn's early light, What so proudly we hail'd at the twilight's last gleaming? Whose broad stripes and bright stars, thro' the perilous fight, O'er the ramparts we watch'd, were so gallantly streaming? And the rockets' red glare, the bombs bursting in air, Gave proof thro' the night that our flag was still there. O say, does that star-spangled banner yet wave O'er the land of the free and the home of the brave?

On the shore dimly seen thro' the mists of the deep, Where the foe's haughty host in dread silence reposes, What is that which the breeze, o'er the towering steep, As it fitfully blows, half conceals, half discloses? Now it catches the gleam of the morning's first beam, In full glory reflected, now shines on the stream: 'Tis the star-spangled banner: O, long may it wave O'er the land of the free and the home of the brave!

And where is that band who so vauntingly swore That the havoc of war and the battle's confusion, A home and a country should leave us no more? Their blood has wash'd out their foul footsteps' pollution. No refuge could save the hireling and slave From the terror of flight or the gloom of the grave: And the star-spangled banner in triumph doth wave O'er the land of the free and the home of the brave.

O thus be it ever when free-men shall stand Between their lov'd home and the war's desolation; Blest with vict'ry and peace, may the heav'n-rescued land Praise the Pow'r that hath made and preserv'd us a nation! Then conquer we must, when our cause it is just, And this be our motto: "In God is our trust!" And the star-spangled banner in triumph shall wave O'er the land of the free and the home of the brave!

—Francis Scott Key, 1814

1

"ALMOST INCREDIBLE VICTORY!"

"GENTLEMEN, THE BRITISH ARE BELOW THE CITY! WE MUST FIGHT FOR THEM TONIGHT."

— General Andrew Jackson in a speech to his troops before the Battle of New Orleans

Major General Andrew Jackson received a warning, in Spetember 1814, from the secretary of war James Monroe. New Orleans was the Royal Navy's next target. Jackson, the commander of the American troops in the West, was watching the enemy from Mobile, Alabama, another possible target. Monroe sent a second warning in October of that year. He was certain the British would attack New Orleans and soon. Jackson wasted no time. He marched west.

The general covered some 350 miles (563 km) in eleven days "to have a view at the points at which the enemy might make a landing."[1] When he arrived in New Orleans on December 1, the general's clothing "was . . . nearly threadbare. A small leather cap protected his head, and a short blue Spanish cloak his body, whilst his high dragoon boots were long innocent of polish . . . his complexion was sallow and unhealthy; his hair iron grey, and his body thin and emaciated."[2] However, his appearance did not detract from the fierce expression of his "bright and hawk-like" eyes.[3] Since the citizens of New Orleans had done little to prepare against invasion, they welcomed Jackson warmly—even in the pouring rain.

Jackson Takes Command

With confidence and energy, Jackson quickly took charge. He studied the few existing maps and spent two days inspecting the surrounding area on horseback. He soon realized that the small forces available to him could not cover all the approaches to New Orleans. Jackson decided to block as many routes as possible. All available men were put to work felling trees across the bayous, the many small waterways leading into or near the city. Jackson needed to work fast. Scouts reported the British were on the way.

Jackson strengthened Fort Saint Phillip, which guarded the Mississippi River south of the city. He added a thirty-two-pound cannon (a cannon that

When an army paymaster held back the wages of nonwhite soldiers, Jackson reprimanded him curtly, saying that wages were to be paid promptly "without inquiring whether the troops are white, black, or tea."[4]

fired thirty-two-pound cannonballs) and ordered the construction of two batteries, fortifications equipped with heavy guns, on opposite banks of the river to provide a crossfire.

Jackson also gathered food and other supplies for battle. What he needed most arrived on December 11, when the steamboat *Enterprise* docked in New Orleans. Its commander Henry Miller Shreve had come all the way from Pittsburgh towing barges of ammunition.

Jackson was critically short of manpower. His next step was to recruit troops from the local population. He drafted a collection that included Creoles, people of French ancestry born in

Louisiana; Frenchmen who had served in the army of Emperor Napoleon Bonaparte of France; Choctaw Indians led by Chief Push-Ma-Ta-Ha; free blacks from Santo Domingo in the West Indies; and the infamous pirates, the Lafitte brothers. Jackson appointed Jean Lafitte as an aide-de-camp. The pirate was extremely familiar with the swampy area the Americans needed to defend.

Andrew Jackson's final defensive move was to send five gunboats under the command of Captain Thomas Catesby Jones to patrol Lake Borgne. This large shallow bay southwest of New Orleans stretched from the Gulf of Mexico almost to the Mississippi River.

British Target New Orleans

In the spring of 1814, the British decided to invade New Orleans. This was not a new idea. Months before, Admiral Alexander Cochrane of the British Royal Navy had told his superiors, "...the Americans are vulnerable [in] New Orleans."[5] Winning control of the Mississippi would be a step to claiming the Louisiana Purchase and eventually all the territory to Canada's border.

On November 26, 1814, a British fleet sailed from Jamaica, an island in the Caribbean Sea, en route to the American port of New Orleans near the mouth of the Mississippi River. Major General Sir Edward Pakenham, a well-respected English hero and soldier, was in command. He was aided by three other major generals: John Keane, Sir

Samuel Gibbs, and John Lambert. Aboard the sixty vessels were 14,000 soldiers and hundreds of government officials—tax collectors, printers, and secretaries. They would be needed to set up a new colony for Great Britain along the Mississippi River. Army officers even brought their wives. Nobody aboard doubted that the ladies would need their silk gowns for the victory ball in New Orleans.

However, the British had a surprise waiting for them. Andrew Jackson, whose toughness had earned him the nickname "Old Hickory," had his defenses in place and promised to "drive their enemies into the sea, or die trying."[6]

Gunboats Patrol Lake Borgne

On December 13, 1814, Captain Jones spotted the British fleet as it dropped anchor in the Gulf of Mexico near Lake Borgne. He immediately sent word to his commander, who relayed the information to Jackson. Then Jones stationed his flotilla at the mouth of the lake to see what the British would do next. He did not have to wait long. The very next day, a line of enemy barges advanced toward the five gunboats crewed by 185 Americans. Outnumbered and outgunned, Jones decided to retreat. Unfortunately, the wind and tide were against him and the flotilla became grounded in deep mud. Jones's choices were to blow up his boats to keep them from being captured by the British, or to make a last stand. He decided to fight. When the skirmish was over, ten

Americans had been killed, thirty-five wounded, and the others taken prisoner. Not one man had escaped to warn Jackson that the British now had a clear route into New Orleans.

As the British interrogated prisoners, Jones and his crew exaggerated the size of Jackson's militia to 20,000. Cochrane did not believe all Jones reported, but he did overestimate the size of Jackson's army. However, the British had no respect for the fighting abilities of the American militia. They expected to win easily. This attitude worked in Jackson's favor.

Capturing the gunboats allowed the British to advance across the lake unopposed, but it was not a simple task. Lake Borgne was too shallow for the fleet's large ships. The British were forced to row 2,000 men 60 miles (97 km) across the lake. It took three trips to transport the men. Several more trips were required to pick up equipment and supplies needed by the soldiers.

Up "Welcome" Bayou

On December 23, Colonel William Thornton, in command of 1,600 British soldiers, landed on the western shore of the lake and rowed up Bayou Bienvenue, which means "welcome." Apparently, Jackson's orders had been disobeyed—the waterway was not blocked. Thornton captured the American troops stationed on a plantation owned by Jacques Villeré only 8 miles (13 km) outside New Orleans. Villeré's son, Gabriel, held captive in his own home, jumped from a window when his guards grew careless, and raced toward New Orleans to warn Jackson.

Fortunately for the Americans, while the British had been rowing troops across the lake, more than 4,000 reinforcements, backwoodsmen from Tennessee and Kentucky, had arrived in New Orleans. These men dressed in homespun clothes and coonskin hats were armed with long rifles, weapons more accurate at long range than the traditional muskets carried by the British soldiers.

After being warned by the panting, mud-stained Villeré, Jackson made the decision to attack the British that night. One hour later, Old Hickory set out with 1,800 men. The rest of the army would follow the next day. The fourteen-gun schooner USS *Carolina* and the twenty-two-gun USS *Louisiana* glided down the Mississippi to support the infantry. It was already dark when the Americans reached the edge of the Villeré plantation. No one made a sound as the troops took their positions.

Certain that it was too late for the Americans to organize an attack, the exhausted British troops were bedding down for the night. They were completely surprised when the USS *Carolina* opened fire. A British officer described the scene: "Flash, flash, flash, came from the river; the roar of cannon followed, and the light of her own broadside displayed to us an enemy's vessel at anchor near the opposite bank, and pouring a

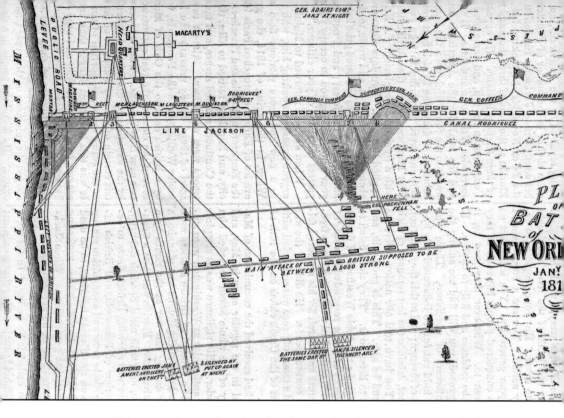

This map shows the plan for the Battle of New Orleans, which would be fought in January. You can see Jackson's line labeled in the top third of the map, running from the cypress swamp to the river.

perfect shower of grape and round shot, into the camp."[7]

Jackson waited a full half-hour while the USS *Carolina* shelled the British camp, then ordered his foot soldiers to attack. Again the British were unpleasantly surprised. The battle continued until midnight when Jackson signaled his men to pull back. By that time, the British had suffered 275 casualties and the Americans 215. Though indecisive, the skirmish left Old Hickory with one important advantage—the British never completely recovered from their shock and surprise. In fact, Jackson's daring attack convinced them that they faced an American force of 15,000 instead of only 1,800. The British decided to wait for reinforcements.

The delay gave Jackson time to prepare. He pulled his troops back to a dry drainage ditch and began to construct a breastwork, a mound of mud and earth to block the British advance. His troops constructed a 5-foot-tall (1.5-m) wall of earth and cotton bales, placing artillery batteries at intervals along its length. The work went on through the night. As one group slept, others dug with picks, shovels, bayonets, and bare hands. Only the general stayed on duty all night. This fortified position protected the American gunners and riflemen from British fire. The wall also had a 4-foot (1.2-m) deep ditch at its foot. Attackers would need ladders to climb to the top. By sunrise, a mound of mud .75 mile (1.2 km) long stretched from a cypress swamp in the east to the Mississippi River in the west. The line was drawn.

Reinforcements!

British General Pakenham arrived on Christmas Day, 1814, with strong reinforcements, but did not press on toward New Orleans immediately. He decided to bring heavy guns from the fleet, to combat the deadly American cannon power. The cannons also had to be rowed 60 miles (97 km) across the lake. During the next few days and nights, the British Navy transported twelve cannons across Lake Borgne. When the bayou narrowed, the guns had to be lifted and dragged through mud and reeds to the road leading to the Villeré plantation. One boat turned over on the lake and seventeen soldiers carrying shot in their packs sank to the bottom and drowned.

On January 7, two regiments of the British Army decided to parade. They marched within sight of the American line. One British soldier recorded, "[t]he music played, the sun shone brilliantly, and every member of two regiments was in the highest of spirits of his chance of being led forward to attack."[8]

By January 6, 1815, 6,000 soldiers and a plentiful supply of ammunition had been transported across the lake. Pakenham was ready to launch his assault on New Orleans.

The Final Battle

On January 8, 1815, the Battle of New Orleans began about dawn when Colonel William Thornton ferried 600 British regulars across the Mississippi. His goal was to seize artillery manned by a force of 700 ill-trained Americans on the west bank. Once the British soldiers controlled the guns, they could be turned on Jackson's main force across the river.

Pakenham had issued his attack orders the night before, but while he slept something went wrong. He had planned for Thornton's troops to cross the river while it was dark, but by five in the morning, the brigade had not left the east bank. It was dawn before Thornton seized the American guns, and he had no time to use them before Pakenham ordered a rocket fired, signaling the main assault.

Under the protection of fog, 5,300 British regulars advanced across the Villeré plantation toward Jackson's main line, defended by 4,700 men. Then the fog lifted. The British troops were completely exposed to American fire.

The Americans started firing grape and canister shot when the British were 500 yards (457 m) away. At Jackson's orders, the drummers behind the American lines beat out "Yankee Doodle."[9] Riflemen opened fire when the distance closed to 300 yards (274 m). The British kept marching. All along the battle line the Redcoats (a nickname earned by the bright red uniform jackets the British wore) were mowed down before they could get near the American breastwork. Only one small column near

Riding his white horse along the American battle line, General Andrew Jackson rallied his troops during the final stage of the Battle of New Orleans.

Struck by a cannonball, British General Pakenham died during the Battle of New Orleans.

the river got through to the American line, but they were quickly driven back by heavy gunfire. Many battle-hardened British soldiers turned and fled. According to one veteran of the European wars fought against Napoleon, it was "The most murderous [fire] I ever beheld before or since."[10]

Pakenham did his best to rally his men as he rode back and forth across the battlefield. One horse was shot out from under him, and shortly after mounting another he was "cut asunder by a cannonball."[11]

General John Lambert, who took command after Pakenham was killed, called for an immediate retreat. The battle had lasted only half an hour but one eyewitness described the field as "a terrible sight to behold, with dead and wounded laying in heaps—all dressed in scarlet

British uniforms."[12] More than 2,000 British soldiers had been killed, wounded, or captured. The United States lost about 70 men.

Ironically, this battle should not have been fought. On December 24, 1814, in Ghent, Belgium, American and British diplomats had signed a treaty ending the War of 1812. However, the official documents, sent by ship, did not reach the American or British forces until weeks after the Battle of New Orleans.

Despite not actually affecting the outcome of the war, this final battle of the War of 1812 did give Americans a victory to celebrate and created a strong spirit of nationalism—a relatively new idea for the young United States. It also made Andrew Jackson a hero. In winning the Battle of New Orleans, Old Hickory had defeated one of the mightiest invasion forces ever assembled at that time.

When the news reached Washington, headlines in the *Daily National Intelligencer* read in boldface: "Almost Incredible Victory!"[13]

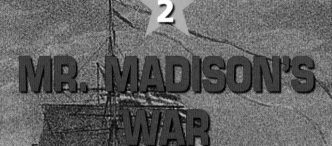

2

MR. MADISON'S WAR

"WHENSOEVER HOSTILE AGGRESSIONS...
REQUIRE A RESORT TO WAR, WE MUST MEET
OUR DUTY AND CONVINCE THE WORLD THAT WE
ARE JUST FRIENDS AND BRAVE ENEMIES."

— Excerpt from a letter by Thomas Jefferson to
Andrew Jackson dated December 3, 1806

On June 18, 1812, the British Ambassador to the United States Augustus John Foster wanted information. Weeks before, Speaker of the House, Henry Clay, had told Foster war was coming. The ambassador still hoped war could be prevented. However, both houses of the American Congress had spent the last two weeks in secret session. With the doors of Congress closed to him, Foster knew the best place to hear the latest political news. He climbed into his carriage for a ride along Pennsylvania Avenue.

He was on his way to the finest house in Washington City, the president's home. On Wednesday afternoons, Dolley Madison, the President's wife, opened her door to everyone. Foster knew members of Congress would be there and would know the subject of the secret talks.[1]

When Foster arrived, he spotted Henry Clay. Clay and other members of Congress were cheerful, and "all shaking hands with one another."[2] Mr. Madison stood to one side, quietly watching the celebration.

Foster and the president talked briefly. The subject of war was not mentioned. However, by the end of the party, Foster felt certain rumors of war were true.

The very next day, American Secretary of State, James Monroe called Foster to a meeting. Monroe presented Foster with the Declaration of War signed by President Madison.

JAMES MADISON,
4ᵗ PRESIDENT OF THE UNITED STATES.
PHILADELPHIA.
Published by C. S. WILLIAMS, N.E. corner of Market & 7ᵗ St.

Madison was Thomas Jefferson's Secretary of State before he became the fourth US president in 1809.

Attack at Sea

The United States officially declared war on Great Britain for the first time in June 1812. However, a confrontation between the USS *Chesapeake* and the British man-of-war HMS *Leopard* pushed America to the brink of war nearly five years earlier.

On June 22, 1807, the USS *Chesapeake* set sail from Norfolk, Virginia. Ten miles (16 km) from port, in American-controlled waters, James Barron, commander of the American ship, watched as a British ship, the HMS *Leopard,* approached. Barron thought he had nothing to fear when a British officer requested permission to board the USS *Chesapeake*. He allowed the officer to board. But the situation quickly changed. The British officer demanded to search the USS *Chesapeake*, claiming that four deserters from the Royal Navy might be on board. Barron knew he had deserters among his crew and wanted to protect them. He ordered the officer off the ship. A short time later, a cannon from the HMS *Leopard* fired . . . and then another, and another. Barron was caught off guard. America was not at war with Great Britain, and he was not ready to fight a sea battle.

Twenty-one cannonballs tore into the USS *Chesapeake's* hull. Its masts were toppled and sails shredded. During the brief battle, three American sailors were killed and eighteen wounded, including Barron. The USS *Chesapeake* surrendered. After the British removed the four deserters, the American ship was allowed to limp back to port.

Americans were up in arms over this attack. Many demanded war. If Jefferson could have asked for a declaration of war, the whole country would have backed him. However, the president decided to avoid war. He believed the country was unprepared for another conflict. Almost five years would pass before James Madison, as president, would officially ask Congress to declare war on Great Britain.

Napoleon and the Royal Navy

The War of 1812 has sometimes been called Mr. Madison's War. However, the events that led to this second conflict with Great Britain (the American Revolutionary War was the first) began long before Madison's presidency. The British attack on the USS *Chesapeake* was only one of many issues. In fact, actions taken by Napoleon Bonaparte, emperor of France, indirectly pushed the United States into war.

Napoleon, who was also one of the greatest generals of all time, was determined to build an empire by conquering Europe. By 1797, Spain, Austria, and Prussia (a country that included large parts of present-day Poland and most of Germany) had been forced to sign peace agreements with France. Napoleon's armies had also occupied Holland. Only Great Britain, which had been at

Here the officers on the USS Shannon *are surrendering to the crew of the HMS* Leopard.

war with France since 1793, continued the fight—struggling to keep Napoleon from conquering its homeland.

Great Britain had survived because the Royal Navy, which was stronger than the French fleet, protected it. The island kingdom would remain safe as long as Great Britain could control the seas. That meant keeping the ships well manned. However, this was not an easy task. Conditions aboard ships in the Royal Navy—poor food, hard work, and harsh discipline—caused British sailors to desert by the thousands. Many chose to work instead on American merchant ships, where the pay and working conditions were much better.

Some British seamen applied to be naturalized citizens of the United States. Many deserters wanted to be recognized as American citizens immediately, and bought "protection papers," fake documents (not issued by the United States government) that could be purchased for as little as one dollar. The British, however, refused to recognize these papers, or any form of naturalization, stating: "Once an Englishman always an Englishman."[3] The Royal Navy was authorized to "impress," which meant taking British deserters from American ships that were stopped on the high seas. Sometimes "mistakes" were made and American citizens were impressed instead. This issue, among others, would eventually force President James Madison to propose war.

Caught in the Middle

During the first several years of war against France, Great Britain did not interfere with American trade. Then, on May 16, 1806, Great Britain proclaimed a blockade of the European coast, stating that no nation could sell goods used for war to France, its colonies, or the countries under French control. Napoleon struck back with the Berlin Decree on November 21, 1806, blockading the British Isles. A series of British Orders in Council followed. One issued on

November 11, 1807, declared that all vessels trading with places from which British ships were excluded were subject to capture unless they first put in at a British port and paid a fee.

On December 17, 1807, Napoleon proclaimed that any vessel submitting to a search by an English ship, or paying a fee to the British government, would be liable to seizure by the French Navy. Neutral commerce could not be pursued without violating one of these orders. The United States was caught in the middle. Between 1807 and 1812, the two warring countries seized about 900 American ships.

Great Britain controlled the seas. British warships waited outside every American seaport and stopped and searched ships. If French-made goods or goods bound for Europe were found, the ship and its cargo were sold at the British naval base in Halifax, Nova Scotia, Canada—a British colony at that time.

Though it had no military power to back any protest, the United States objected to the search and seizure of its ships. Great Britain and the United States also disagreed on the definition of blockade, on articles listed as contraband, on what areas of a ship should be searched when it was stopped, and the impressment of sailors from American vessels.

Embargo Act of 1807

Though war fever had spread in America after the attack on the USS *Chesapeake*, Thomas Jefferson, the president in 1807, first tried to solve the problem through diplomatic channels. He wrote to James Monroe, his minister in London, England, and directed Monroe to demand not only the return of the seamen taken from the USS *Chesapeake,* but also "the entire abolition of impressment from vessels of the United States."[4]

When Great Britain refused, Jefferson decided to try economic pressure. He recommended that Congress pass the Embargo Act of 1807, halting United States trade with the whole world. This act made it illegal for an American vessel to sail to any foreign port and banned all European vessels from United States seaports. Jefferson believed that Great Britain's economy would be hurt if the United States, the largest consumer of British manufactured goods, refused to buy from it. The United States was also the world's largest neutral carrier. By refusing to transport goods to England, France, or their colonies, Jefferson hoped to cripple the British and French war efforts.

The embargo had little effect on the British. However, it did bring the American economy to a near standstill, and almost put the country's merchant marine out of business. It also succeeded in turning regions across the country against one another. In the southern states and western territories, many citizens supported the embargo. They believed that Great Britain was treating them like unhappy colonists instead of citizens of an independent country. New Englanders, who depended on the shipping industry, nearly declared civil war because they were so angered by the embargo. Jefferson finally had to admit that the Embargo Act was a failure. In March 1809, after it had been in effect for fifteen months, Congress repealed the embargo. It was replaced in 1809 by the Non-Intercourse Act, which allowed Americans to trade with all nations except Great Britain and France.

The British and the Native Americans

Americans also took issue with the British on one other front. Before 1776, colonists homesteading in Indian Territory west of the Allegheny Mountains had been discouraged by England. The policy was not to protect the lands of American's native tribes, but to make it easier for Great Britain to control the valuable fur trade.

After the United States became an independent country, even the threat of Indian attacks did not keep settlers from moving west and settling on the rich lands of the Northwest Territory (an area that eventually became the states of Ohio, Illinois, Indiana, Michigan, Wisconsin, and part of Minnesota). By 1810, American Indian raids were increasing on settlements in the Northwest Territory. Most settlers believed the uprisings were "instigated and supported by the British in Canada."[5] In fact, Great Britain's defeat in the Revolutionary War did

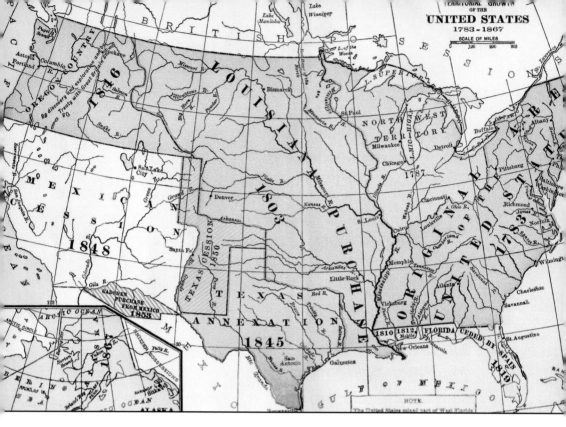

This map depicts the United States as it looked around the time of the War of 1812. The Northwest Territory is near the Great Lakes.

not end its friendship with American Indians. The British wanted to keep the profitable fur trade for themselves. The richest source of these furs was the Northwest Territory, and Great Britain continued to encourage the tribes to resist the stream of American settlers moving into the area.

Tensions had been mounting since 1805, when two Shawnee brothers—Tecumseh, a great orator, and Tenskwatawa, known as "The Prophet," a spiritual leader—began organizing an Indian confederacy. The Shawnee leaders established their camp at Prophet's Town along the Tippecanoe River in northwestern Indiana. Tecumseh dreamed of an Indian confederacy stretching from Florida to Lake Erie—a confederacy strong enough to resist white settlers. He traveled great distances speaking to the tribes of the Kickapoo, Wea, Creek, Wyandot, Sauk, Fox, Potawatomi, Miami, Choctaw, Osage, and others.

The settlers in the Indiana Territory became increasingly fearful of Tecumseh's power. They knew the Shawnee chief would drive them out when he felt strong enough, and asked for protection from the United States government before it was too late.

William Henry Harrison, governor of the Indiana Territory, was determined to crush Tecumseh's Indian confederacy. In November 1811, while Tecumseh was on a recruiting mission in the south, Harrison moved 1,000 soldiers into position across the Tippecanoe River from Prophet's Town. The Prophet ignored Tecumseh's orders—to avoid war with Harrison at all cost—and prepared for battle, promising his 2,000 warriors an easy victory. He told them that he had placed a spell on the white soldiers, making them too weak to defend themselves. The Prophet ordered his band to kill Harrison, the white leader who rode a gray horse.

On the morning of November 7, a sentry posted near Harrison's camp spotted Indians and opened fire. Normally, the warriors would have moved forward slowly, hiding behind trees and large rocks. However, The Prophet's vision had foretold an easy victory, so the Indians charged the camp. Harrison's troops easily drove them back three times. When the Indians discovered that The Prophet had deserted them, they panicked and fled. Later that day, Harrison ordered Prophet's Town burned to the ground. The Battle of Tippecanoe ended Tecumseh's dream of an Indian nation, but did little to stop the Indian uprisings on the frontier. Many soon returned to Prophet's Town. In fact, by June 1812, Harrison noted that the force there was as strong as the previous summer.

The Battle of Tippecanoe encouraged tribes to keep fighting the American settlers moving into the Northwest Territory. The Shawnee chief Tecumseh and hundreds of followers joined forces with British troops. They made their way to Fort Malden in Canada, where the British welcomed them. Tecumseh made camp there and waited for the big war that he knew was coming.

In April 1812, Henry Clay addressed Congress, stating "he had no doubts that the late Indian War on the Wabash was executed by the British."[6] There was no truth to this statement, but it added fuel to the talk of war.

Congress Votes for War

When President James Madison took office in 1809, he hoped for peace. The shipping centers of New England and New York resented the search and seizure of their ships but preferred that to a war, which would destroy overseas trade altogether.

The South and West, however, continued to resent the way Great Britain was treating the United States. They believed that free trade, sailors' rights, and the chance to end the Indian uprisings forever were worth fighting for. Many of the newly elected representatives from these regions quickly earned the name "War Hawks." They believed the United States would have to fight to earn Great Britain's respect.

The War Hawks, led by Speaker of the House of Representatives Henry Clay, convinced Madison to demand that the British revoke the Orders in Council. This was the act that excluded neutral vessels, like those of the United States, from ports where British ships were banned. In March 1812, Madison sent a written demand to Great Britain on the USS *Hornet*. The ship returned on May 19 without a positive response from the British government. On May 22, Madison began composing his war message. On June 1, the message was submitted to Congress. In it, Madison outlined several American grievances: impressment of sailors, the search and seizure of American ships by British warships, blockades as defined by the Orders in Council, and the renewal of Indian warfare in the western territories.

The president declared that Britain had carried out "a series of acts hostile to the United States as an independent and neutral nation…American citizens…have been torn from their country and from everything dear to them."[7]

On June 4, the House of Representatives passed the Declaration of War by a vote of 79 to 49. On June 17, the Senate voted 19 to 13 in favor of war. President James Madison signed the Declaration of War the next day—June 18, 1812. A Boston paper, the *Independent Chronicle,* supported the decision, saying that British policies had threatened the American merchant, seaman, and frontiersman. The United States was forced... "either to surrender their independence, or maintain it by War.[8]

A Second War for Independence

The British, who had temporarily stopped Napoleon's advance in Europe, did not want war. British-Canadian settlers did their best to stay out of it, and most Americans had no desire to fight. However, the British had pushed the Americans too far. Through continued indifference to the young country's pride, Great Britain had repeated many of the errors that had led to the Revolutionary War. In that sense, the War of 1812 was a continuation of the American Revolution.

What Americans did not know, as they prepared for war, was that the Non-Intercourse Act had been working. By the early months of 1812, the economic effects of the embargo were being felt in Great Britain. British politicians realized that they needed American trade and called for the suspension of the Orders in Council.

The Orders were suspended on June 16, 1812, two days before the United States declared war, but the news arrived far too late. It had to be sent across the Atlantic on a sailing ship—a trip that routinely took four to six weeks.

In fact, news of the declaration of war did not reach London until July 30, 1812. For a time, the British expected a speedy end to the war since the Orders in Council were repealed. This was not to be. Americans also insisted acts of impressments must end. The British refused to compromise on that issue.

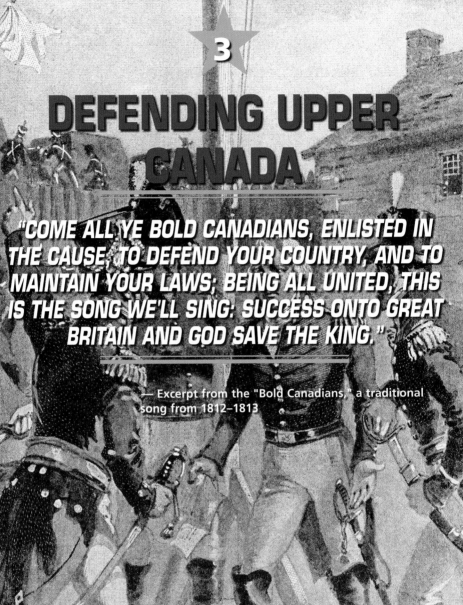

3

DEFENDING UPPER CANADA

"COME ALL YE BOLD CANADIANS, ENLISTED IN THE CAUSE, TO DEFEND YOUR COUNTRY, AND TO MAINTAIN YOUR LAWS; BEING ALL UNITED, THIS IS THE SONG WE'LL SING: SUCCESS ONTO GREAT BRITAIN AND GOD SAVE THE KING."

— Excerpt from the "Bold Canadians," a traditional song from 1812–1813

The British and Canadian troops stationed along the border of Upper Canada were under the experienced command of General Isaac Brock. Brock was delighted once the Americans declared war. He expected to stop any invasion, winning glory for himself.[1] Brock gathered troops on the Canadian side of Lake Ontario and hurried to reinforce Fort Malden in the settlement of Amherstburg (now Windsor).

Since the British Royal Navy controlled the Great Lakes, Brock's troops traveled by water. On August 13, his force reached Amherstburg and joined their Indian allies led by the "extraordinary character" Tecumseh. Tecumseh and his warriors were camped in an open field near Fort Malden. Shouts and cannon shots woke them. The noise, a welcoming salute for Isaac Brock, came from the deck of the HMS *General Hunter.* The Indians fired muskets in their own salute.

Though the hour was late, Brock invited Tecumseh and other chiefs to meet with him. Brock and Tecumseh liked and respected each other at once. After thanking the Indians for their welcome, he said: "I have fought against the enemies of our great father, the king beyond the Great Lake and they have never seen my back. I am here to fight his enemies on this side of the Great Lake and now desire with my soldiers to take lessons from you and your

TECUMSEH.

Tecumseh would help the British in several battles during the War of 1812 before being killed by the Americans in 1813.

warriors so that I may learn how to make war in these great forests."[2]

Brock wanted to attack Detroit immediately. His officers wanted to wait. Tecumseh supported Brock's plan. The warrior "unrolled a long peel of birch bark on the table, fastened its corners with stones, and drew a map of the area with the tip of his scalping knife. Brock watched with admiration as Tecumseh sketched in roads, streams, hills, and ravines."[3]

As the two leaders planned the attack on Fort Detroit together, the Shawnee chief earned the British commander's respect. Brock reported that "a more sagacious [wise] or more gallant warrior does not exist."[4]

Advantage Lost

During the winter of 1812, before the declaration of war, William Hull visited Washington. He asked President Madison for command of the Northwestern Army. He had a plan. Hull wanted to invade Upper Canada from Fort Detroit. He believed this would reduce the threat of an Indian attack, and "probably induce the Enemy to abandon the province of Upper Canada without Opposition."[5] Madison approved Hull's plan, gambling on his leadership and experience. Hull had commanded troops during the American Revolution.

In April 1812, General Hull, age sixty, arrived in Dayton, Ohio, to take command of 2,000 troops. It had been decided that the British-Canadian forts and towns in the Great Lakes region would be the first targets in the event of war. Hull was to reinforce Fort Detroit in the Michigan Territory—a post located along the United States' northern boundary.

On June 1, the troops began the march north. In 1812, the trail that connected Dayton, in southwestern Ohio, to Detroit led through the Black Swamp. To transport artillery, supplies, and themselves over the area, Hull's troops had to build a road. They also had to keep a constant watch for Tecumseh's spies who observed the army's slow advance.

By June 24, Hull's army had covered only half the distance, reaching Fort Findley in northwest Ohio. There, the general received a letter from Secretary of War William Eustis, dated June 18—the very day that war was declared. However, the message simply ordered Hull to advance as quickly as possible to Detroit and wait for further orders.

Hull and his troops hurried on, but the swampy trail continued to slow their progress. Then on July 1, the general found a small American ship, the USS *Cuyahoga*, moored along the Maumee River that flowed north to Lake Erie. He decided to ship his cannons and heavy equipment to Fort Detroit, rather than continuing to haul them over land. Still unaware that the country was at war, Hull also loaded a trunk of his confidential military papers aboard.

Meanwhile, the dispatch to General Hull, informing him that the United States was at war, had been delayed. It had been misplaced in the Cleveland post office.[6] Finally, after several hours of searching, the document was found in the Fort Detroit mailbag and a courier was dispatched immediately. He galloped through rough terrain for more than three days and delivered the news to Hull on July 2 at two in the morning. After reading the dispatch, the general sent a boat to try to catch the USS *Cuyahoga*, but it was too late. Later that day, the British, who had learned four days earlier that war had been declared, captured the USS *Cuyahoga* and Hull's papers.

On July 5, Hull marched into Detroit, a settlement of about one hundred fifty houses on the outskirts of the log fort. He was prepared to cross the river into Canada and attack Fort Malden, which was manned by a small force— until he learned of the USS *Cuyahoga's* capture.

Now that the British had vital information about his plans and the strength of his force, Hull lost his confidence and his best opportunity to take the British-held fort. He decided to fortify his position at Detroit, establish a dependable supply route, and forage for flour, blankets, whiskey, sheep, and cattle. However, the delay would be fatal. It gave Brock and his Indian allies time to mount an attack.

Brock Takes Fort Detroit

On August 15, as Chief Tecumseh and his warriors surrounded the American fort, Brock sent a message to Hull demanding "the immediate surrender of Detroit."[7] When the American general refused, British warships began firing their cannons across the wide river. Outside the fort, people ducked behind doors and scrambled for safety as cannonballs hit their homes. One man had just gotten up from bed when a shot came through the room and struck his pillow. Another cannonball smashed through the center of the table as a family sat around it, then dropped through the floor, and into the cellar. The bombardment continued until well after dark.

Inside Fort Detroit, the cannon fire seemed to have unnerved General Hull. His aide found him crouched on an old tent that was lying on the ground. The general was chewing tobacco furiously, adding more and more, sometimes removing a piece, rolling it between his fingers, then replacing it.

Brock accepts William Hull's sword as a symbol of his surrender of Fort Detroit. Tecumseh stands to the left of Brock.

The American troops wanted to return fire, but Hull was too frightened and upset to organize a plan. Six men had died already, several more were wounded, and the shelling continued. On August 16, 1812, Hull surrendered without having fired a shot. "Not an officer was consulted," said one witness. "Even the women were indignant at so shameful a degradation of the American character."[8] The general was later court-martialed and found guilty of cowardice.

Under the terms of the surrender, General William Hull gave up Fort Detroit and its contents—all the ordnance (weapons and ammunition), the supplies, and its troops. The Americans stacked their arms and moved out. Then the British and Canadians entered the fort, pulled down the Stars and Stripes, and hoisted the British Union Jack in its place.

In addition to the loss of Fort Detroit, two other American posts fell to the British and their American Indian allies during the summer of 1812. Fort Michilimackinac on Mackinac Island was taken on July 17 after the British moved a cannon to a hill overlooking the fort during the night. Outnumbered at least ten to one, the Americans were forced to surrender.

After the loss of Fort Michilimackinac, Hull, as commander of the Northwestern Army, ordered the evacuation of Fort Dearborn, near Chicago, Illinois. Though a friendly chief warned Captain Nathan Heald not to leave the protection of the

Fort Dearborn was built in 1803. After the massacre there, the Native Americans burned the fort to the ground. This shows the fort after it was rebuilt.

fort, the captain felt he must obey his orders. On the morning of August 15, about 100 soldiers and civilians, including a wagon train of women and children, set out for Fort Wayne in Indiana. Only a few miles from Fort Dearborn, 500 Potawatomie Indians attacked the group. Most of the party was killed. Twenty-nine soldiers, seven women, and six children were taken captive.

With the fall of these three forts, only Fort Wayne in the Indiana territory remained in American control. The whole northwest was now unprotected. Many settlers in outlying areas abandoned their homes for the relative safety of blockhouses, small log forts built in towns to provide a refuge during an attack.

More Lost Battles in Canada

While Brock's attention was focused on Fort Detroit, Stephen Van Rensselaer was appointed commander in chief of the New York militia, though he had no previous military experience. He moved troops into position near Fort Niagara in western New York State. Fort Niagara faced a Canadian post, Fort George, across the Niagara River that connected Lake Ontario to Lake Erie. By October 1812, 6,000 American troops were stationed along the border near Fort Niagara, and Brock feared that the Americans would attack soon. He quickly moved most of his troops to Fort George.

Before daybreak on October 13, 600 American troops landed in Canada near the village of Queenston and opened fire. Shots could be heard 6 miles (9.6 km) downriver at Fort George, and Brock hurried to the battle scene. For a while, it looked as if the Americans would be victorious. By two o'clock, Van Rensselaer's troops controlled the strategic hill that overlooked the area. Then, Brock was mortally wounded as he led an assault to recapture the hillside, but not before he ordered General Roger Sheaffe to march from Fort George with every available man.

With more British and Canadian troops on the way, Van Rensselaer called for reinforcements.

However, for reasons unknown, the soldiers refused to cross the river. Without additional troops, the Americans were soon hopelessly outnumbered and another battle was lost.

In November 1812, American General Henry Dearborn, age sixty-one (and so feeble that his troops nicknamed him "Granny") led betweem 6,000 and 8,000 troops north along the shores of Lake Champlain. His goal was to capture Montreal, a Canadian town on the St. Lawrence River. On the night of November 19, American troops seized a blockhouse held by a small Canadian force near Plattsburgh (now located in New York State). The enemy soldiers escaped. However, in the dark, the Americans became confused, fired on one another, then pulled back. Four days later, Dearborn and his army retreated. With that final fiasco, all plans to seize Canada in 1812 ended.

Causes for Defeat

When war had been declared five months earlier, the freshman congressman John C. Calhoun declared that "in four weeks . . . time . . . the whole of Upper and a part of Lower Canada will be in our possession."[9] The United States government felt confident of a victory. The British, who had to defend a border some 1,700 miles (2,736 km) long with fewer than 8,000 troops, were significantly outnumbered.

As with the events that led to the War of 1812, the reasons that the United States was so unprepared to fight had begun much earlier. In the 1790s, the political group called the Federalists controlled Congress. This group believed that the best way to preserve American neutrality was to be prepared for war. By 1801, the Federalists had increased the army from 840 men to 5,400 and the navy to thirteen medium-sized warships called frigates, with six more under construction. They also began building a system of coastal forts to protect American cities from assault by sea.

In 1801, the opposing political party, the Republicans, took office. Republicans were determined to cut defense spending. Within a year, the army was trimmed to 3,300 men, construction on ships was halted, and most of the frigates were decommissioned, or removed from service. The Republicans did spend money on coastal forts, but without a navy to act as a first line of defense, most seaport cities were an easy target for attack from the sea.

Madison Gets Blamed

After declaring war in 1812, the United States was soon confronted by several problems caused by this lack of preparedness. The regular army was undermanned and had little training and even less battle experience. State militias, from which the government hoped to draw additional troops, would not get involved unless the state itself came under attack. The United States Treasury did not have enough money to cover all its war expenses.

The system of paying troops broke down from the beginning. As the war progressed, army pay was often six to twelve months late. The supply system was inefficient. Troops in the field frequently had to go for months at a time without shoes, clothing, blankets, or other vital supplies. The procedure for feeding the troops was even worse. The daily ration was supposed to consist of twenty ounces of beef or twelve ounces of pork; eighteen ounces of bread or flour; four ounces of rum, brandy, or whiskey; and small quantities of salt, vinegar, soap, and candles. The food the troops received was often spoiled and the portions smaller than promised.

However, the fundamental causes for the defeats suffered by the United States were poor tactics and leadership of generals recruited because of their experience during the Revolutionary War. Now old and feeble, these leaders were recruited because younger officers lacked experience and were unable to control the men in their command.

By the end of 1812, the United States Army was in shambles. Thousands of American soldiers and settlers had died. The Northwest Territory was more dangerous and disorganized than ever. Most of the Michigan Territory was in British hands. In fact, the boundary of the American frontier had been pushed back to the Ohio River (a boundary the Indian tribes considered the border between white territories and their own lands). Many

Indians, who had been reluctant to fight on either side, were now committed to the British. The British retained control of the Great Lakes, and the population of Canada, which had been drawn reluctantly into war, was now fired by enthusiasm over Brock's stunning victory.

After six months of fighting, the outcome of the war looked bleak, and Congress blamed Madison for not appointing better, more experienced, officers.

AMERICA'S NAVY TAKES THE SEAS

"IF YOU WISH TO AVOID FOREIGN COLLISION, YOU HAD BETTER ABANDON THE OCEAN."

—Speaker of the House of Representatives
Henry Clay in a speech given January 22, 1812

When war was declared in June 1812, the role of the American Navy was almost over-looked. The first plan was to use the small United States Navy as floating batteries—sites for heavy guns—to defend American ports. They also hoped to capture or de-stroy some of the British cargo ships carrying supplies bound for Canada. With the defeat of the American Army in Canada, the Navy's role changed.

During the last ten years, the Republican controlled Congress had refused to spend money on the navy. When war broke out the American fleet had only sixteen ships. Seven were frigates. The USS *Constitution*, *President*, and *United States* were outfitted with forty-four cannons. The USS *Constellation*, *Chesapeake*, and *Congress* had thirty-eight big guns, and the USS *Essex* had thirty-two. The other nine ships had fewer guns. The navy also had about 200 small gunboats.

Early in 1812, the Secretary of Navy, Paul Hamilton, asked for funds to expand the country's fleet. He wanted ten new frigates and twelve ships of line. Even the possibility of war did not loosen Congress's purse strings. They turned Hamilton's request down. Only funds to refit three frigates were provided.

The British fleet, the largest in the world, had more than 600 vessels. How could the much smaller American Navy challenge its warships for control of the Atlantic Ocean? It seemed like an impossible feat.

However, the small American Navy had several factors working in its favor. The frigates, built in the 1790s, were well constructed. Even after twenty years of service, the ships were considered the most powerful of the time. Their officers and men were also well-trained sailors and skilled marksmen with cannons and small arms. They had gained experience against French and Spanish privateers off the shores of the Mississippi Delta.

Unlike the conditions in the army, food and other provisions were more than adequate. The navy's small size made it easier to supply, and once a frigate was outfitted, it could remain at sea for months.

Sailor's pay was also better. Before the war, seamen earned ten to twelve dollars a month; skilled gunners earned eighteen. However, in 1812, to attract new recruits, the navy began offering incentives. If seamen signed on for two years, they received a bounty, or bonus, ranging from ten to thirty dollars and three months' advance salary. Monthly pay was also increased by 25 percent. Morale on board ships was high and sailors were prepared to follow their captains into battle. And they did, with results that lifted the spirit of the country.

Hull and the USS *Constitution*

During June 1812, Captain Isaac Hull, commander of the forty-four-gun USS *Constitution*, prepared to sail from Annapolis, Maryland. Hull, an experienced seaman, had first gone to sea when he was fourteen. However, most of his crewmembers were new recruits. The captain trained and drilled the 450 men almost day and night. Then at noon on July 4, after firing a fifteen-gun salute in honor of the nation's birthday, he sailed. His orders came directly from Secretary Hamilton. The USS *Constitution* was to sail to New York and join the USS *United States,* *President,* and *Congress.*

On the afternoon of July 17, the *Constitution's* lookout spotted topsails on the horizon. Hull was wary at first. He knew the Royal Navy ships would be positioned along the coast. However, it seemed more likely these were the ships he had been assigned to join. By 10 o'clock that night, the ships were only about 6 miles (9.6 km) away. Hull ordered signal lanterns raised to confirm the others' identity. When the coded signal was ignored, Hull ordered his ship to turn about. The USS *Constitution* was sailing into an enemy squadron.

At dawn, Hull considered the odds. Two British frigates were almost within cannon range. The others were close behind. Hull was outnumbered. Then the situation worsened. "Soon after Sunrise, the wind entirely left," Hull explained later in a report, "and the Ship would not steer." The USS *Constitution* could not fight or run. To Hull it "appeared

In the battle that was to come, the USS Constitution *would earn the nickname "Old Ironsides."*

we must be taken, and that our Escape was impossible."[1]

In the coming hours, Hull was determined to prove himself wrong.[2] He ordered two boats lowered to tow the ship. The oarsmen strained to pull the fully loaded 2,200-ton ship away from her pursuers. The British followed suit, using more boats and oarsmen. They soon began to gain on the USS *Constitution*. Next Hull lightened his load. He ordered casks of freshwater emptied over the side.

The British continued to close the gap. By eight o'clock, four enemy ships were dangerously close. Hull's situation looked desperate. "It...appeared we must be taken," he wrote.[3] But no matter the odds, he would not surrender. He intended to fire as many broadsides as he could and go down fighting.

As a last resort, Hull ordered his crew to try kedging the ship. Kedge anchors were carried ahead in the ship's boats and dropped in shallow water. The ship was then reeled in toward the anchors. This final trick worked. Hull watched as the distance grew between the USS *Constitution* and the British frigates.

The next morning Hull reported, "only three of them could be seen from the Mast head, the nearest of which, was about twelve miles off directly astern."[4]

Only hours before, the British Commodore smelled victory. He was so confident he would overtake the USS *Constitution*; he had picked the prize crew "to have the honor of sailing the *Constitution* to Halifax."[5] Hull and his crew had outsmarted British's finest for two and a half days.

The USS *Constitution* reached Boston Harbor safely on July 26. The story spread quickly, and Captain Isaac Hull was praised.

A Victory at Sea

Hull feared that the British fleet would soon blockade Boston Harbor. He worked his crew for twelve hours—without relief—to load supplies on board his ship. By August 2, the USS *Constitution* was at sea again. After sailing about 750 miles (1,207 km) from port, Hull's crew sighted the HMS *Guerriere*, commanded by British Captain James R. Dacres. Immediately, both captains prepared for battle and tried to gain the advantage by positioning their ships. For forty-five minutes, Hull and Dacres sailed around each other, each trying to turn sideways and fire his cannons first, but neither could outmaneuver the other.

Finally, Dacres opened fire. His first shots fell short. He made a half-circle and fired again. This time his shots were too high, and Hull made his move. He raised more sail and closed quickly on the HMS *Guerriere.* The American sailors on the USS *Constitution* held their fire until the ship pulled within 50 yards (46 m) of the British vessel. Then Hull gave the order: "Now boys, pour it into them."[6]

CONSTITUTION & GURRIERE.

The British ship HMS Guerriere *was destroyed in the fight with the USS* Constitution.

Within fifteen minutes, the HMS *Guerriere's* mizzenmast, the mast nearest the stern of the British ship, toppled. The hull and sails were badly damaged. The British crew fought bravely, but after two more masts fell, Dacres surrendered.

During the battle, an American seaman saw a cannonball bounce off the USS *Constitution's* side and exclaimed: "Huzza, her sides are made of iron."[7] From then on, the ship was nicknamed "Old Ironsides."

The crew worked through the night to remove prisoners from the HMS *Guerriere* and tend the wounded. The badly damaged British ship was set on fire. Hull sailed back to Boston with his prisoners. His victory at sea encouraged Americans to believe they could win the war. It was much-needed encouragement. Only a few days later, news of General William Hull's surrender at

Detroit reached the East Coast. (Isaac Hull was William's nephew.)

The US Navy Sets Sail

Isaac Hull's victory also brought an end to the plan to keep the American Navy close to its home ports. President Madison and his cabinet members now realized that the nation's fleet could be effective at sea. By September 7, 1812, the ships were divided into three squadrons under the command of Captains John Rodgers, Stephen Decatur, and David Porter. New orders were issued. The navy's primary role was to protect American merchant ships as they sailed the high seas. However, the captains were also instructed to pursue whatever course needed to annoy the enemy while protecting United States commerce. The skillful American captains set sail immediately to meet this challenge.

Captain Stephen Decatur, commander of the USS *United States,* preferred to sail solo and separated from the other ships in his squadron soon after leaving port. On October 25, about 600 miles (965 km) west of the Canary Islands, off the coast of Africa, Decatur and his crew encountered Captain John S. Carden and the recently overhauled British frigate, HMS *Macedonian.* When the two ships sighted each other, the wind was blowing in favor of the British ship. By maintaining its course, the HMS *Macedonian* could have closed quickly on the USS *United States,* nicknamed "The Wagon" since it was so difficult to sail. However, the British frigate had fewer cannons. Carden first made the mistake of keeping his distance, and then foolishly made a hasty approach.

Decatur responded in a cool, calculated manner. He outmaneuvered his foe, and then fired so many cannons at the same time that the British crew thought the USS *United States* was on fire. By the time the HMS *Macedonian* got within 100 yards (91 m), its masts and sails were shot away. One-third of its crew was dead or wounded. A British sailor described the damage done by the American guns: "the large shot came against the ship's side, shaking her to the very keel, and passing through her timbers and scattering terrific splinters, which did more appalling work than the shot itself."[8]

As Decatur positioned the USS *United States* to fire again, Carden surrendered. Decatur placed part of his crew aboard the HMS *Macedonian.* They sailed for Newport Harbor in Rhode Island with the British prisoners on board. This was the first and only time a British frigate was brought into an American port as a prize of war.

The USS *Essex* Raids the Pacific

In December 1812, Captain David Porter decided that he would annoy Great Britain by attacking its whaling vessels in the Pacific Ocean. When his ship, the USS *Essex*, rounded Cape Horn at the southernmost tip of South America in March 1813, it became the first American warship to sail the Pacific. The USS *Essex* hunted for several months. It seized fifteen ships and an estimated "two and one half million dollars worth" of sails, cables, anchors, provisions, medicines, and other stores.[9] This nearly destroyed England's whaling industry before ships from the Royal Navy could reach that corner of the ocean.

In February 1814, the British did finally corner Porter and the USS *Essex* at Valparaiso, Chile. For a month, the British blockaded the harbor. Then as Porter tried to make a run for open sea, a storm toppled his topmast. He was forced to drop anchor. He tried to reach neutral waters near shore, but the British moved in and attacked. The USS *Essex* was quickly destroyed. Three-fifths of the crew were killed, wounded, or drowned. This defeat ended American sea power in the Pacific and made it possible for the Royal Navy to target American fur posts on the Columbia River (the border between the present-day states of Oregon and Washington) and the American whaling industry in the South Seas.

Privateers Capture Cargo

The victories of the American Navy were significant, but even more important was the role of what one Republican called our "cheapest and best Navy"—American privateers.[10] As soon as war was declared, privately owned vessels of every description took to the high seas to prey on the British merchant marine. These privateers cruised the coast of Canada and islands in the Caribbean Sea, hoping to seize goods from British ships that could be sold at a huge profit. In the first six months of war, their captains and crews captured 450 ships. The USS *Yankee*, sailing out of Bristol, Rhode Island, seized eight British vessels valued at $300,000, and the USS *Rossie* out of Baltimore, Maryland, took eighteen enemy ships worth close to $1.5 million dollars.

Navy Frigate Captured!

One more important sea battle occurred outside Boston Harbor in June 1813. Captain James Lawrence, who had taken command of the USS *Chesapeake* on May 18, was ordered to put to sea "as soon as the weather and force and position of the enemy [would permit]."[11] Two British frigates were prowling at the mouth of the harbor.

On June 1, 1813, the USS *Chesapeake* sailed. Shortly after leaving the safety of Boston's harbor, Lawrence sighted the British frigate HMS *Shannon*, and ordered his crew to prepare for battle. Lawrence gained the first advantage. He was positioned to cut across the HMS *Shannon's* stern and fire. However, for an unknown reason, he did not seize this opportunity. Instead, he moved in for a close-range duel. This made it possible for expert British gun crews to fire into the open

American gun ports. It took only three British broadsides to wipe out most of the USS *Chesapeake's* crew and seriously wound its captain. As Lawrence was carried below, he gave the famous command that became the motto for the American Navy: "Don't give up the ship."[12]

After the British boarded the USS *Chesapeake,* the Americans continued to fight for a brief time, then surrendered. One hundred Americans were wounded and seventy were killed, including Captain Lawrence, in this fifteen-minute battle. The USS *Chesapeake* became the first American frigate to be captured by a British ship during the war.

The defeat of the *USS Chesapeake* stirred the navy into action. More boats were needed to defend the coast. Joshua Barney was appointed to build twenty gunboats to do the job. Barney spent the next few months building the special flotilla and training recruits. The USS *Chesapeake* squadron needed to be ready when the British returned.

Lawrence is being carried below decks after being mortally wounded in the battle with HMS Shannon.

A Victorious Year

In 1812, the war at sea gave the United States' morale a much-needed boost, especially after the fall of Fort Detroit. The British were stunned by their defeats, even though the loss of a single ship, here and there, to the United States Navy did not significantly reduce the Royal Navy's strength. Attitudes in London began to change. The United States had earned respect.[13]

However, by 1813, Great Britain had no plans to end the war. They began to build heavy frigates equipped with more cannons, and its warships already at sea were ordered not to cruise alone or to engage in single combat with American ships.

British naval forces were also instructed to do something to bring the war to America. By May, American ports from Long Island to the Mississippi River were blockaded. Only along the New England coast were ships able to come and go at will. Many citizens in that part of the country made their living from the sea. They were calling for an immediate end to the hostilities. Great Britain hoped to encourage the New England citizens' demands. The British blockade also trapped the United States Navy in port and put an end to American victories at sea for the duration of the war.

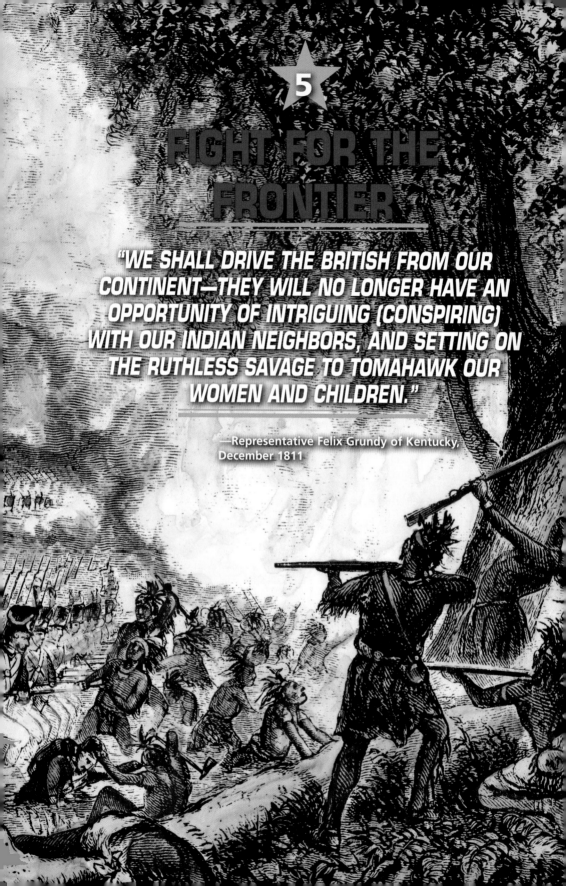

5

FIGHT FOR THE FRONTIER

"WE SHALL DRIVE THE BRITISH FROM OUR CONTINENT—THEY WILL NO LONGER HAVE AN OPPORTUNITY OF INTRIGUING (CONSPIRING) WITH OUR INDIAN NEIGHBORS, AND SETTING ON THE RUTHLESS SAVAGE TO TOMAHAWK OUR WOMEN AND CHILDREN."

—Representative Felix Grundy of Kentucky, December 1811

The American defeat at Fort Detroit on August 16, 1812, did not mean President Madison was giving up. He was even more determined than ever to invade Canada.[1] Madison was a fighter at heart though he had never served in the military. The president's first task was to find a new commander for the militia in the Northwest Territory, some-one who could take command and lead an army to victory.

Secretary of State Monroe volunteered for the job, but Henry Clay and the War Hawks suggested another candidate. They pressured Madison to appoint William Henry Harrison.[2] They believed that Harrison's defeat of The Prophet and his warriors at the Battle of Tippecanoe in 1811 proved that he could lead troops to victory.

Madison had another good reason to select Harrison. The thirty-nine-year-old Virginian was very popular in Kentucky. On August 25, 1812, the Kentucky legislature made Harrison a major general. He was not a citizen of that state, but they put him in charge of the 5,500 volunteers in the Kentucky militia. With Harrison as the new commander in chief of the Northwestern Army, Madison hoped Kentuckians would sign on for the fight. And they did. Unlike many eastern states, where it had been difficult to raise an army, when the Kentucky governor called men to arms, more volunteered than were needed.

Harrison soon learned that British troops were marching toward Fort Wayne in the Indiana Territory, burning houses, destroying crops, and killing livestock along the way. Three hundred Indians reportedly had surrounded the fort. Harrison and the Kentucky militia marched north immediately. With only eighty men, the commander of Fort Wayne, James Rhea, could not hold out for long.

When the troops reached Dayton, Ohio, Harrison received a letter from Secretary of War John Armstrong telling him that he had been appointed a brigadier general in the United States Army. However, if Harrison accepted this appointment, he would serve under Brigadier General James Winchester, who had been commissioned six months earlier. The sixty-one-year-old Winchester had earned a reputation fighting Indians in Tennessee, but he was not as popular in the West as Harrison. Like William Hull, Winchester appeared older than his years and unsure of himself. Plump and graying, he had to have help mounting and dismounting his horse. In contrast, thirty-nine-year-old Harrison was vigorous, decisive, and totally confident. In a return letter to Washington, D.C., Harrison suggested that the backwoodsmen "would never perform anything brilliant under a stranger," meaning Winchester.[3]

Not waiting for further word, Harrison and 3,000 men pressed on to Fort Wayne. By September 12, his force had warded off the enemy without firing a shot. Five days later, President Madison appointed Harrison commander in chief of the Northwestern Army—a force expected to grow to 10,000 with all the regulars and volunteers from Kentucky, Ohio, Indiana, Pennsylvania, and Virginia. Winchester would now serve under Harrison's command.

Taking Command

The commander's first order of business was to defend the frontiers and retake Detroit. To control Great Britain's Indian allies, he sent mounted troops to burn their villages and destroy their fields of corn, beans, and pumpkins, denying them food and shelter. The Potawatomi and Miami Indians escaped to Canada and joined the British.

To retake Detroit, Harrison divided his army into three forces. General Simon Perkins marched his brigade toward Sandusky, Ohio, on the west end of Lake Erie. Units from Pennsylvania and Virginia were to join him there. Perkins was instructed to build three blockhouses near Sandusky and construct a 15-mile (24-km) road across the Black Swamp to the Maumee rapids. A second group of 1,200 soldiers, under the command of Brigadier General Edward Tupper, was to follow the road Hull had built, stockpiling provisions in blockhouses along the way. The final force, under the command of General Winchester, was to approach the Maumee rapids from Fort Defiance (near present-day Defiance, Ohio). The three columns were to meet at the rapids, then march on to Detroit.

However, Harrison soon faced problems similar to the ones that had plagued Hull. The autumn rains made it impossible to transport the heavy guns, ammunition, and rations for an army of 10,000 across the swampy route. He was forced to make camp well south of the Maumee rapids. Troops under Perkins's command did get cannons to Upper Sandusky by December 10, but at an enormous cost. Many supply wagons were abandoned. Teams of horses, exhausted from pulling through deep mud, had to be destroyed.

Harrison was finally forced to wait for the winter freeze, when the army could transport baggage and artillery across the frozen rivers and along lake shores. While they waited, Harrison's troops were often without enough food, proper winter clothing, and medical supplies. The British controlled the easiest supply route through the Great Lakes. All supplies for the American Army had to be transported overland. Private contractors hired to handle supplies frequently delivered insufficient quantities, and what little was received was often spoiled.

In addition, there was still no adequate way to fund the war effort. New taxes were unpopular and Congress postponed passing a bill to raise money. Even Henry Clay and the other War Hawks had agreed to the delay. They wanted to get on with the fighting.

Some positive changes had been made, though. Secretary of War Armstrong had advanced talented young officers to positions of leadership. The troops were better trained. Bounties and increased pay had attracted more volunteers. By the spring of 1813, there were about 30,000 men in uniform—more than twice the number at the beginning of the war—though most were still inexperienced.

Rout at Frenchtown

Though all the forces of the Northwestern Army were short of supplies, the 1,200 Kentucky troops under Winchester suffered the greatest hardships that autumn. They slept in crude huts and survived on half rations—when they had food at all. Surprisingly, few quit.

Finally, on December 20, 1812, Harrison ordered Winchester to march toward the Maumee rapids. En route, Winchester received word that American settlers in Frenchtown along the Raisin River (near present-day Monroe, Michigan) needed to be rescued. Reportedly, a considerable quantity of food was stored there. In desperate need of supplies and bored by months of waiting, the troops voted to send a small force.

On January 18, 1813, Colonels John Allen and William Lewis, with 660 men, crossed the frozen Raisin River and surprised the enemy pickets. The British and Indians fell back, fighting every foot of the way, but by evening, the American troops controlled Frenchtown. General Winchester arrived two days later with 300 additional troops.

With his claim of victory, Winchester grew careless. The next day, his scouts warned him that British troops from Fort Malden were headed for their camp. However, Winchester did not believe the report was accurate. He ignored it. The commander settled in, enjoying the small comforts the frontier village offered. He took over a house, put on his nightshirt, and slept peacefully until

two hours before dawn. Cannon shots woke
Winchester. He pulled on his uniform and watched
helplessly as Indian sharpshooters picked off 100
of his troops.[4]

Troops led by British General Henry Procter,
commander at Fort Malden, immediately opened
fire with artillery. Then, 1,200 British regulars and
Indians charged. The Americans retreated in
confusion. Only the Kentuckian militia held out,
firing back from the cover of a split rail fence. The
British captured Winchester and ordered him to
force his troops to surrender. At first the troops
from Kentucky refused to put down their guns,
shouting defiantly.[5] They surrendered only after
the British had promised safety for the prisoners
and good treatment for the wounded.

Colonel Procter marched back to Fort Malden
that same day, taking prisoners who could walk.
Arrangements were made to transport about
thirty wounded Americans to the fort early the
next morning. Procter left them under guard.
However, soon after the British left, a number of
Indians, painted black and red and drunk on
captured whiskey, came into town. They set the
houses where the prisoners were being held on
fire. Most of the wounded burned to death. Some
tried to crawl out windows but were
tomahawked, scalped, then pushed back inside.
The treatment of these wounded soldiers was not
forgotten. "Remember the Raisin" was a cry used

to rally the troops to battle during the rest of Harrison's campaign.

Attack Along the Maumee

Harrison was informed of Winchester's defeat when he reached the rapids on January 22, 1813. Without men to replace those lost at the Raisin River, and with the six-month enlistment of many of his militia drawing to a close, Harrison had to call off his winter campaign. Instead, he decided to establish a strong defensive position along the Maumee. He chose a site just below the rapids on the south bank and began building a well-planned fortification. Fort Meigs was exceptionally strong. It was ringed by picket logs, reinforced by mounds of dirt, and protected by blockhouses and batteries that overlooked all approaches.

Meanwhile, prodded by Tecumseh and his followers, Procter assembled an army of 900 soldiers and 1,200 Indians. He knew Harrison was shorthanded and wanted to attack Fort Meigs before American reinforcements could arrive from Kentucky.

On April 28, 1813, one of Harrison's scouting parties reported that between 1,500 and 2,000 enemy troops were camped within striking distance. Tecumseh's Indians had already crossed the river and surrounded Fort Meigs. Harrison was outnumbered more than two to one. His only hope was the 1,500 reinforcements from Kentucky, but would they arrive in time?

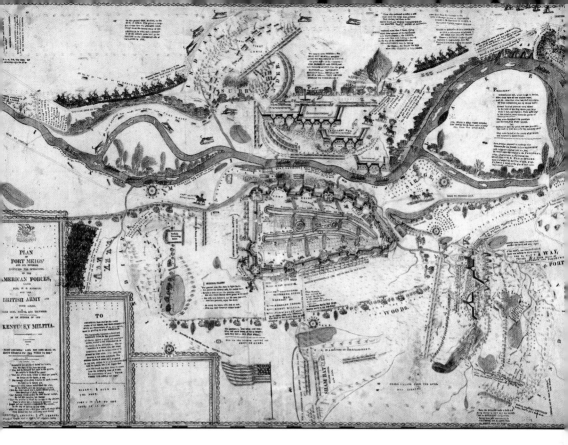

This map shows the position of various troops and groups of Indians during the battle at Fort Meigs.

For three days, Procter bombarded the fort with artillery, firing round after round. He hoped to force Harrison to surrender, but most of the cannonballs fell harmlessly on the dirt mounds surrounding the stockade. Then Harrison received news that reinforcements were only two hours away. He sent orders to them instructing part of the troops to row across the Maumee River, capture the British cannons, drive spikes in the touch holes, destroy the gun carriages, then retreat immediately to their boats. Unfortunately, his orders to retreat were not delivered.

The reinforcements crossed the river and they confronted a band of Indians before reaching their target. After a brief fight, the warriors fled. The Kentuckians then attacked the British battery, driving the gunners off quickly. As they celebrated the easy victory, more Indians appeared at the edge of the woods, and then retreated. Still unaware that Harrison wanted them to row back across the river, the soldiers followed the warriors—and walked into a trap. The British regulars attacked from the front while the Indians closed in behind them. When the skirmish was over, the Indians began to massacre the prisoners. This time, however, Tecumseh restrained his warriors. Observing Procter's indifference to the needless bloodshed, the Shawnee chief reportedly said: "Begone, you are not fit to command, go and put on petticoats."[6]

Twelve hundred of the reinforcements from Kentucky did reach Fort Meigs safely. Realizing that he had lost his best opportunity to seize the fort, Procter abandoned the fight and marched back to Canada on May 4, 1813. During the battle, 320 American soldiers were killed or wounded and 600 captured.

This woodcut engraving shows Tecumseh rebuking Procter for being cowardly.

The British lost only about 100 men, not including their Indian allies. Though the American losses were much greater, the British had not captured the fort, mainly because it was built so well.

Procter tried to take Fort Meigs once more, unsuccessfully, before targeting Fort Stephenson on the Sandusky River. After bombarding the stronghold from gunboats, Procter ordered the regulars to attack. As they marched forward, the British were mowed down by the sharpshooters and "Old Betsy," the fort's one piece of artillery. According to Procter's own account, "the fort, from which the severest fire I ever saw was maintained . . . was well-defended."[7] The 160 Americans led by twenty-three-year-old Major George Croghan held their ground. By August 1813, William Henry Harrison and the Northwestern Army had regained an American foothold along the border.

Tecumseh's Last Battle

The attempts to take Fort Meigs and Fort Stephenson ended Procter's invasion into United States territory, but Procter and his Indian ally, Tecumseh, were destined to meet Harrison once more. In late September 1813, the Northwestern Army marched toward Detroit, only to discover that the British had abandoned the fort. Tecumseh had wanted to stay and fight. He was disgusted by Procter's retreat but followed him east along the shores of Lake St. Clare.[8]

Harrison and 3,500 American troops pursued Procter and Tecumseh across the border. As they advanced, they found baggage and supplies discarded by the British, and captured two gunboats carrying Procter's spare ammunition. Many Indian warriors had disappeared into the forest. Even British soldiers were deserting, leaving Procter with a force of only 1,500.

Harrison caught up with the British on October 5, 1813, at the Thames River, about 40 miles (64 km) east of Detroit. Though badly outnumbered, Procter prepared to fight, arranging his 1,000 soldiers and Tecumseh's 500 warriors in two thin lines between the Thames River and a swamp.

The cavalry, led by Colonel (and Congressman) Richard M. Johnson, asked Harrison for permission to charge the British line. Although this was an unusual plan, Harrison agreed. "The American backwoodsmen ride better in the woods than any other people," he said. "I was persuaded too that the enemy would be quite unprepared for the shock and that they could not resist it."[9]

Shouting "Remember the Raisin!" Johnson's troops galloped toward the enemy. They burst through the enemy line easily, dismounted, caught the British in a crossfire, and forced them to surrender.

However, the Indians continued to fight even against overwhelming odds, urged on by Tecumseh's battle cry. Then, suddenly, something was missing. The troops quickly realized that the voice of the Shawnee chief—whom they hated and feared, yet also admired—had fallen silent. Tecumseh was dead. The Indians withdrew. Exactly fifty minutes after Harrison had ordered the first charge, the battle was over.

Later, Johnson claimed to have killed Tecumseh. Whether he did or not is uncertain. The body of the chief was never found by the white men. The Kentucky troops thought one corpse decorated with feathers and war paint was Tecumseh. They cut strips of flesh from his back and thighs for souvenirs. But they were probably wrong. Chief Tecumseh always dressed simply.[10] What happened to his body remains a mystery. Most likely his warriors spirited him away and buried him in a secret grave.

The Battle of the Thames was a great victory for the United States. Casualties were light and 600 British soldiers were captured. This victory crushed British power in the Northwest. The death of Tecumseh also shattered hopes of an Indian confederacy and the chance to preserve their native way of life in the Northwest Territory.

6

COMMODORE OLIVER HAZARD PERRY

"GIVE ME MEN, SIR, AND I WILL GAIN BOTH FOR YOU AND MYSELF HONOR AND GLORY ON THIS LAKE, OR PERISH IN THE ATTEMPT."

—Captain Oliver Perry requesting additional sailors from his commander on Lake Erie, 1813

By the end of the summer of 1812, the British and Americans agreed on one issue: Lake Erie was the key to winning the war. The balance of power favored the Royal Navy. The British had six ships armed with two to seven guns on Lake Erie. When Isaac Hull surrendered, the United States Navy had lost its one and only frigate on that lake. Five other vessels were bottled up at the eastern end of the lake, by the guns of British-held Fort Erie. The British still used the Great Lakes to move troops quickly from place to place. They ferried weapons, supplies, and food for soldiers and their Indian allies from the Atlantic coast.

It was clear that the United States needed to gain control of lakes Erie and Ontario. There was simply no way to support large armies in the region without free use of the lakes.

In September 1812, President Madison and his cabinet ordered the construction of a Great Lakes fleet and appointed Captain Isaac Chauncey commander in chief. His orders were to "use every exertion to obtain control of them [lakes Erie and Ontario] this fall."[1]

Chauncey first bought merchant ships and outfitted them for war. These vessels were not built to support cannons and would often capsize when the guns were fired. Chauncey needed brigs, large two-masted ships, that were built especially for battle. He assigned a young naval officer, Commander Oliver Hazard Perry, to oversee the construction operation at Presque Isle, on the shores of Lake Erie.

Shipbuilding at Presque Isle

In October, work began on four gunboats and two brigs at Presque Isle (near present-day Erie, Pennsylvania).

Commander Perry arrived to take over supervision of the shipbuilding on March 27, 1813. He was accompanied by his thirteen-year-old brother, Alexander, and 150 seamen. The twenty-eight-year-old immediately focused his attention on completing the work as quickly as possible—not an easy task. Several problems made it difficult to build "modern" fighting vessels hundreds of miles from civilization. Timber—oak, poplar, ash, cedar, walnut and pine—was the only ship-building resource found near Presque Isle. However, there were no sawmills nearby to make planking; all the timber work had to be done by hand.

The USS Niagara *was one of the brigs built by Perry for use in the War of 1812.*

Everything else—anchors, cannons, long guns, canvas for sails, rope for rigging, fittings and tools—had to be brought from Pittsburgh. These supplies were first hauled by keelboat up the Allegheny River and French Creek. The final trek of 41 miles (66 km) was made with oxcarts over roads filled with mud holes and blocked by stumps and fallen trees.

Perry worked at a grueling pace every day and expected everyone else to work just as hard. All his ships needed to be ready to sail into battle before the British attacked Presque Isle.

When construction was completed, these four ships, along with five others stationed at Black Rock on the Niagara River, would give Perry's fleet an edge over the six British ships on Lake Erie.

However, the Black Rock flotilla could not be moved to Presque Isle as long as the British occupied Fort Erie. The fort sat across the river from Black Rock. The American ships would be easy targets if they tried to leave the harbor.

The Capture of Upper Canada's Capital

While Perry was overseeing the building of the fleet, Chauncey took command of the naval forces at Sackets Harbor on Lake Ontario. His orders from Secretary of War John Armstrong were to attack the Canadian post of Kingston along the St. Lawrence River. York, near the west end of Lake Ontario, was the next target, then finally forts George and Erie along the Niagara River.

Chauncey soon mistakenly reported that 6,000 men guarded the Kingston garrison. Fearing that the 4,000 men at Sackets Harbor would be insufficient to carry out the original plan, Chauncey and the commander of the army, General Henry Dearborn, convinced Armstrong that York should be the navy's first goal.

In April 1813, Chauncey sailed from Sackets Harbor. His fleet included his flagship, the new 24-gun USS *Madison*, the 18-gun USS *Oneida*, and twelve other smaller armed ships. Aboard were 1,700 troops under the command of General Zebulon Pike, a young officer who had already gained fame as an explorer. The American force landed west of York, the capital of Upper Canada, on April 27. Supported by Chauncey's fleet, Pike's force advanced with little opposition, seized the batteries guarding the harbor, and pushed on along the lake toward the garrison and the Canadian government buildings.

Within 400 yards (366 km) of the garrison, Pike halted and ordered his men to stand their ground until gunners could drag the heavy artillery into position through the mud. Knowing that victory was his, Pike sat down on a stump to wait until everything was ready for the final attack.

Then the ground shook. A gigantic roar filled the air as the garrison burst into flames. Chunks of masonry, broken beams, boulders, rocks, and stones of every size rained down on the American troops, killing or injuring more than 100 men. Major General Sir Roger Hale Sheaffe, the temporary governor-general of Upper Canada had decided to retreat without a fight. He wanted to save his troops. To prevent the Americans from claiming the naval stores at York, he had blown up the main magazine, the storehouse for all the ammunition.

Pike was mortally wounded. As surgeons carried the general from the field, the British Union Jack was hauled down and the Stars and Stripes raised. The Americans had won. But the price was high—320 Americans died, mostly due to the explosion of the garrison's magazine.

During the victory celebration that followed, the legislative building was set on fire—reportedly by American soldiers and sailors after they found a scalp (which may have only been a wig) hanging in one of York's government buildings. No one is certain who the culprits were. Some Canadians may have been involved.[2] It was never Chauncey's policy to have public or private buildings burned.

The same group was blamed for looting houses in the area, but without any hard evidence. Some historians suggest that the culprits were individual American sailors, not wearing military uniforms. However, the myth that the Americans burned the capital gained acceptance along the Canadian frontier as time passed, and created a strong feeling of hostility toward the United States.

Zebulon Pike was asked by Thomas Jefferson to explore the southern portion of the Louisiana Purchase, made in 1803. He was killed during the Battle of York during the War of 1812.

The capture of York was an important victory for the United States. One British ship was destroyed and a large quantity of naval stores seized. This helped equalize British and American forces on Lake Ontario. It also hindered Royal Navy operations on Lake Erie, as one British officer reported, since the "ammunition and other stores for . . . Lake Erie were either destroyed or fell into enemy's hands when York was taken."[3] Finally, the raid on York was the first in a series of campaigns that eventually allowed Perry to assemble his Great Lakes fleet.

British Retreat

One month later, on May 29, British Commodore Sir James Yeo, with 800 regulars, attacked Sackets Harbor. Though most of the American troops were away aiding Dearborn's campaign along the Niagara front, those left to guard the well-fortified post defended their position well. The British force was driven back.

Although the attack failed, the raid was not totally unsuccessful. A young American naval officer burned a large quantity of his own supplies and nearly burned the USS *General Pike*, a new United States ship that was under construction. The officer had been told that the Americans were losing the battle. Meanwhile, on May 27, 1813, an American force attacked Fort George on the shores of Lake Ontario and the Niagara River. Outnumbered and outgunned, the British troops abandoned this post and also evacuated nearby Fort Erie. After the Americans took the Niagara River, Perry was free to gather his flotilla. The ships from Black Rock sailed safely to Presque Isle, arriving just before the British fleet blockaded the harbor.

Clear Sailing for Perry

By July 10, 1813, the gunboats and brigs of the Presque Isle fleet were completed. After hearing about the "Don't give up the ship!" incident, Perry named one of his 480-ton brigs the USS *Lawrence.* The other brig was christened the USS *Niagara.*

Perry's next problem was how to get his large ships over a sandbar at the mouth of the harbor. It had protected the vessels while they were being built. Now, however, the guns had to be removed while the brigs were lifted over this obstacle. Unarmed, the ships could easily be destroyed by the British fleet that was lurking nearby, so Perry decided to wait.

Then, the British relaxed the blockade on August 1, 1813. Captain Robert Barclay sailed to a small Canadian village on Ryason's Creek. Residents had invited him and his crew to a banquet. During the rounds of toasting, Barclay told his hosts why he had left Lake Erie completely unguarded. He stated with confidence, "I expect to find the Yankee brigs hard and fast on the bar at Erie when I return, in which predicament it will be a small job to destroy them."[4]

The very next day, the five smaller American vessels ringed the channel outside Presque Isle Bay, guarding the men who began lifting the two larger boats over the sandbar. Crews attached floats filled with water to the sides of the brigs beneath the waterline. As the water was pumped out and replaced by air, the floats rose, lifting the vessel. It took four days of strenuous labor to lift the USS *Lawrence* and the USS *Niagara* safely over the sandbar.

Now Perry faced only one other problem—he needed sailors. In a letter to Chauncey, he complained about this situation: "Conceive my feelings: an enemy within striking distance, my vessels ready, and not enough men to man them."[5]

On August 10, Perry's problem was partially solved when Jesse D. Elliott, a battle-tested commander, arrived with about 100 experienced seamen and half a dozen officers. Though still short of men, Perry placed Elliott in command of the USS *Niagara*, and on August 12 sailed west to Sandusky Bay to meet with General Harrison. Harrison offered Perry a hundred Kentucky marksmen as crew, though most had never sailed anything larger than a flatboat or raft. However, after Perry explained what to do, the new recruits turned out to be pretty good sailors. With his fleet now fully manned, Perry was now ready to meet the enemy.

Perry Takes the Challenge

As the strength of the American Navy grew on lakes Ontario and Erie that summer, the Royal Navy could no longer depend on supplies arriving by that route. By September, the British at Fort Malden needed food—for themselves and their 1,400 Indian allies. On September 9, 1813, Captain

Barclay, with six ships, made a run to collect supplies from a post on Lake Ontario.

Perry, with his fleet of nine, sighted the Royal Navy ships the next day. Though Perry had more ships, the British still had the advantage because of their long-range guns. Even knowing this, Perry ordered his fleet to sail closer. As they approached the enemy, Perry ordered sand strewn on the decks to prevent the men from slipping on any blood that might spill. He had food served so that the crews would go into battle with full stomachs.

As soon as the USS *Lawrence* was within reach, the British opened fire with their long guns. Perry could not return fire. The distance was too great for his shorter guns. He sailed closer, directly into the enemy fire. The rest of the American fleet lagged behind. The USS *Caledonia* was a slow ship, and Captain Elliott kept the *Niagara* at a distance, using only his long-range guns. After two hours of fighting, the USS *Lawrence* suffered severe damage. Her sides were riddled by shot from all directions. The decks were bloody and covered with bodies. Nearly the whole crew was dead or wounded. All its guns were useless. The British planned to destroy the commodore's flagship and force the American squadron to retreat.[6]

However, instead of surrendering, Perry hauled down his banner with Lawrence's famous words on it, "Don't give up the ship." He jumped into a small boat that had somehow survived the British bombardment, and with his brother and four seamen, rowed toward the USS *Niagara*. In his usual manner, Perry stood in the stern of the boat. The British fired broadsides and small arms at him until the crew pulled him down for his own safety.[7] With shot falling all around him, Perry somehow reached the ship safely and took command. With an undamaged vessel at his command, he sailed back into battle. The USS *Niagara* broke through the British line. The crew fired the portside guns into the HMS *Chippewa, Little Belt*, and *Lady Prevost.* The guns on the starboard side raked the other three British ships, the HMS *Detroit, Queen Charlotte*, and *General Hunter*. Then two of the larger British ships locked together while attempting to turn, and Barclay surrendered.

The battle lasted about three hours. In the end it was a decisive victory. Perry held out against a British squadron that had more guns and men. On the back of an old letter, Commodore Perry penciled his famous dispatch to General Harrison: "We have met the enemy and they are ours: two ships, two brigs, one schooner, and one sloop."[8] This battle finally ended Great Britain's control of Lake Erie.

A Draw not a Victory

During 1813, Napoleon Bonaparte regained his throne as emperor of France and once again pursued plans to expand his empire. Great Britain was again forced to focus on the war in Europe

Perry's nine ships battle the six British ships at Put-in-Bay on Lake Erie.

and its strategy against the United States was to remain defensive. It could not afford to send more troops across the Atlantic Ocean, and the country simply expected the Canadians to hold their own against the Americans.

The British failure to maintain control of the Great Lakes would have serious consequences. The Royal Navy could no longer move men, supplies, and messages quickly and efficiently along the Canadian border. This set in motion events that led to Perry's victory on Lake Erie, the defeat of the British at the Battle of the Thames, and the collapse of the Indian confederacy.

Though the success of Perry and Harrison along the Canadian front in 1813 seemed promising, in reality, these wins simply restored the situation to the way it had been before the war. Also, American attacks on Canadian towns created feelings of hostility and British and Canadian forces soon retaliated by raiding American border towns. The war's final battles were still to be fought.

WASHINGTON UP IN FLAMES

"WAS IT THESE ASHES, NOW CRUSHED UNDER-FOOT, WHICH ONCE HAD THE POWER TO INFLATE PRIDE?...WHO WOULD HAVE THOUGHT THAT THIS MASS, SO MAGNIFICENT, SHOULD IN THE SPACE OF A FEW HOURS BE THUS DESTROYED?"

—Excerpt from a letter by resident Margaret Bayard Smith describing Washington, D.C., after the capital was burned by British forces

On the morning of August 17, 1814, the Point Lookout watchman saw a shocking sight. Fifty British ships were anchored in Chesapeake Bay near the mouth of the Potomac River. The fleet included several warships, each equipped with seventy-four or more cannons. There were frigates, schooners, and sloops of war. Transport ships carried thousands of soldiers. The British Navy had picked its next target—the Chesapeake Bay area.

The bay was the most direct route to Washington and Baltimore. These cities were the center for much of America's shipping and privateering. A large portion of the country's population lived along its coastline. There was little doubt the British planned to strike, but what was their target? Baltimore was the larger and wealthier of the two cities. But Washington would be a unique prize: the capital city of the young country and the home to the US president and Congress.

Only Commodore Joshua Barney and the 500 men of the Chesapeake Bay flotilla, a group of small, armed boats, guarded the waterway that led directly to the nation's capital.

The British Pick a Target

In 1814, Napoleon was finally defeated in Europe by the combined forces of Great Britain, Prussia, Russia, and Austria. This freed thousands of British troops for duty in the war against the United States. Americans had attacked the Royal Navy at sea and tried to take parts of British Canada. With reinforcements, the English planned to give their rude American cousins a "good drubbing."[1]

By June 1814, 4,000 British troops under the command of Major Robert Ross and Royal Navy warships led by Sir Alexander Cochrane had established a base on the Tangier Islands in Chesapeake Bay, within easy striking distance of Washington and Baltimore.

The British commanders debated where to strike, but Cochrane was determined. The target would be the capital city of the United States. Capturing Washington would do the utmost to wound America's pride and shatter morale.

Even with the British perched on their doorstep, President Madison and his cabinet were slow to act. Secretary of War John Armstrong believed Washington was in no danger. He declared: "They certainly will not come here. . . . No! No! Baltimore is the place. . . ."[2]

Major General John Van Ness, commander of the Washington militia disagreed adamantly with Armstrong. He pushed for a strong defense plan. Other senior officers complained also, saying: "The enemy can with a small force destroy Washington in its present situation…sur[e]ly it might and ought to be protected."[3] But nothing was done to defend the coast or stop the enemy from marching on the capital.

It was not until July 1 that President Madison began to take the British presence seriously and finally ordered to have an army assembled to protect the capital.

March Through Maryland

On August 18, the British fleet sailed into Chesapeake Bay. The Americans' only defense was Barney's gunboat flotilla. The flotilla was completely outnumbered by the British ships and forced to retreat.

The next day, four regiments of British regulars and a Royal Navy battalion landed near Benedict, Maryland. They marched north along the Patuxent River. In one deserted town, soldiers found bread baking in ovens,[4] but no militia to offer resistance.

George Cockburn was warned that the American gunboats were about to attack. He set off immediately in pursuit of the small flotilla. When the British cornered Barney and crew, the captain blew up his boats to keep them from falling into enemy hands.

Meanwhile, the main British force marched toward Washington. Their commander, Ross, a veteran of the Napoleonic Wars, had some doubts about this venture. His troops were badly out of shape after the long trip across the ocean. He had no cavalry and only three small field guns. However, no one blocked the road or burned any bridges to slow the British advance. It was not until after Ross and his troops had marched 14 miles (22.5 km) to Bladensburg, Maryland, that they began to see any signs of American resistance.

Too Little, Too Late

On August 22, 1814, when the British had advanced to within 16 miles (26 km) of Washington, Madison and his cabinet finally realized the danger. News of the landing had reached Brigadier General William Winder, commander in chief in the Washington area, five days earlier. Since then, he had been frantically trying to raise an army to fight the British. Though Winder should have had 15,000 men under his command, only 3,000 were actually available— since the government would not call on them until the danger was "imminent."

On August 24, Winder spent most of the predawn hours riding the countryside trying to devise a plan. When his horse gave out, he stumbled about on foot, fell into a ditch, and hurt his right arm and ankle. For a while, the general's own aides could not find him and feared that he had been captured by the British.[5] Winder gained little useful information during this misadventure. By morning, he was still uncertain of where the British planned to attack. He ordered Brigadier General Tobias Stansbury, with 2,000 militiamen, to occupy Bladensburg, Maryland. Brigadier General Walter Smith and 1,500 District of Columbia militia were to wait at the Potomac Bridge on the eastern outskirts of Washington, ready to march where needed. The only experienced troops available that August morning were a handful of regulars and 400 naval men, the crew of the Chesapeake flotilla.

At ten o'clock, Winder's scouts finally brought him the information he needed. The British were advancing on Bladensburg. Winder immediately ordered Smith to march with his troops to reinforce Stansbury. An hour later, General Winder, the president, and most of the cabinet followed them.

Stansbury's untrained troops formed two lines on the hills above Bladensburg, overlooking the town bridge. Sharpshooters and cannons were on the frontline, while other troops formed a second line some distance back. Another regiment also took position to the left of the frontline—until Secretary of State James Monroe, who had always wanted to command the American forces, ordered it back .25 miles (.4 km). This new position was too far away to be useful, but by the time Winder arrived to inspect the lines, it was too late to make any changes. One mile (1.6 km) to the rear, Smith's brigade formed a third line as the troops arrived from Washington.

President Madison, dressed in black with two borrowed dueling pistols at his waist, Attorney General Richard Rush, and the secretaries of state, war, and the treasury all gathered near the lines. However, when a scout who had been sent to watch for signs of the British galloped back to announce the enemy's approach, he discovered the presidential party out in front of the American lines, riding toward Bladensburg. The scout warned President Madison and his cabinet to retreat to safety.

Retreat!

Shortly after noon on August 24, the fighting began. The American cannons and sharpshooters fired relentlessly as the British troops marched across the bridge at Bladensburg. Many British soldiers were killed or wounded. However, with so many men, as soon as one British soldier fell, there was another who stepped forward and took his place in the battle line.

The British easily pushed the American sharpshooters back. Then General Ross began firing off rockets, and the inexperienced, untrained American militia that formed the two frontlines panicked and fled. The rockets, long tubes filled with powder, worked like fireworks. They completely missed their marks, but made a terrifying sound.

The third American line, Washington's final defense, held out a bit longer before retreating. Only the naval veterans under Commodore Joshua Barney stood their ground until they were out of ammunition. Barney, badly wounded, made sure that most of his men escaped before he surrendered to the British.

Soon the road to Washington was filled with retreating Americans. Fortunately, the president and cabinet had already galloped back toward the city. Madison knew the threat to the capital was grave. He stopped once to write a brief note to the his wife. He told Dolley to be ready to leave the city "at a moment's warning… The British… were marching on the city, with intentions to destroy it. She should make her arrangements to pack what papers she could and escape."[6]

Dolley Madison

The First Lady had spent the morning peering out the windows of the president's house. She turned her spyglass in every direction, hoping to catch a glimpse of her husband. No sign of Mr. Madison, but what she saw concerned her. Soldiers wandered aimlessly in the streets, unarmed and seemingly unprepared to "fight for their own firesides."[7]

By three o'clock in the afternoon, Mrs. Madison was still waiting for word from the president. She listened to the boom of the cannons and watched the rockets flash across the sky as she wrote a letter to her sister: "Will you believe it, we have had a battle near Bladensburg, and I am still here within sound of the cannon! Mr. Madison comes not. May God protect him! Two messengers, covered with dust, come to bid me fly; but I wait for him."[8]

As the messengers had galloped up to the president's house, one had shouted: "Clear out, clear out! General Armstrong has ordered a retreat!"[9]

Dolley Madison had earlier ordered her carriage loaded with trunks that contained the cabinet's official papers. She watched calmly now as the silver, books, more papers, a small clock, and even the mansion's red velvet curtains were loaded into a wagon. She took time to add this to the letter to her sister: "Mr. Carroll has come to hasten my departure and is in a very bad humour because I insist on waiting until the large picture of George Washington is secured, and it requires to be unscrewed from the wall."[10] They finally had to take apart the frame to remove Washington's portrait. Finally, the First Lady of the United States climbed into her carriage, but only after she was sure the Washington canvas was safe.

By this time, the streets of the capital city were crowded with soldiers, government officials, women, and children in carriages, horses, wagons, and carts loaded with household goods, all trying to escape before the British attacked by fleeing across the wooden bridge on the west side of the city.

Dolley Madison is famous for saving this portrait of George Washington painted by Gilbert Stuart.

Banquet and Bonfires

On the evening of August 24, Ross and Cockburn, with two British regiments, marched into a deserted Washington, D.C. Unopposed by any American troops, the British set fire to the Capitol and the Treasury buildings. They helped themselves to an abandoned banquet at the Madisons—a victory dinner ordered by the

This image shows the Capitol building after the British set fire to it.

president earlier that morning. Then, the British burned the president's house.

The next day, public buildings and private homes valued at more than a million dollars were burned. The fires burned until torrential rains began to fall later that night. Gale-force winds blew roofs off already damaged houses. Several buildings toppled, burying British soldiers in the debris. Two cannons were lifted from their mounts and hurled several yards. Discouraged by the violent storm, Ross ordered his troops back to their ships on the evening of August 25, 1814, leaving behind the charred remains of the capital of the United States.

Reclaiming the Capital

Following the disastrous defeat, General Winder abandoned the capital and retreated as far as Montgomery Court House, 12 miles (19 km) north of Washington. There, he tried unsuccessfully to collect his army. Meanwhile, President Madison, the First Lady, and the cabinet members were wandering about the countryside for two days looking for each other. It was not the US government's finest hour. If the president had taken the threat on the capital seriously, he would have had a plan in mind to reconvene with his advisors.

On the evening of August 27, after receiving a note from Monroe stating that the British had left the capital and were returning to their ships, the president rode back into Washington. He found the president's house a roofless shell and saw that "the roof, that noble dome [on the House of Representatives], painted and carved with such beauty and skill, lay in ashes in the cellars beneath the smouldering ruins."[11] Even as he surveyed the damage, Madison heard more cannon fire followed by a dreadful explosion. The British had attacked and blown up Fort Washington, located on the Potomac River just outside the city.

The Madisons moved into a home that the British had not destroyed. The president and his cabinet began reorganizing the government. Secretary of War Armstrong, who was blamed for this disaster, resigned. Monroe temporarily took over the War Department. On September 20, 1814, the third session of the Thirteenth Congress began its work in a crowded room in the Post Office Building. Its first task was to demonstrate that the government was once again in control of the nation's capital and that it would continue to function.

Rockets' Red Glare over Baltimore

While the president and his cabinet were preoccupied in Washington, the British lost no time launching an assault on Baltimore. Their plan was to strike from land and sea.

Unlike the city of Washington, Baltimore was prepared for the British. Maryland's Governor Winder had started preparations in May. He knew Fort McHenry in Baltimore Harbor needed improvements. He appointed Major George Armstrong as the fort's new commander. Armstrong immediately set to work adding more big guns. He also built additional batteries to guard the entrance to the harbor.

These improvements to the fort's structure were not all Armstrong wanted. He wanted something to raise the city's morale.[12] He asked for a huge flag that would fly over his fort and could been seen for many miles.

This flag was made by a Baltimore woman, Mary Pickersgill, and her thirteen-year-old daughter, Caroline. The giant banner measured 42 feet by 30 feet (13 x 9 m). The fifteen stars were 2 feet (.6 m) from point to point. Each red and white stripe was 2 feet (.6 m) wide. Mary and her daughter needed 400 yards (366 m) of strong bunting for the project. They also needed a large area to spread out. An ale house let them work on its floor. For several weeks, mother and daughter spent long hours cutting and stitching. By August, Armstrong had his flag.

On September 12, Sir Alexander Cochrane and the Royal Navy anchored 14 miles (22 km) outside the city. British General Ross and 4,500 men disembarked. While the general marched north, the fleet sailed on toward its target—Baltimore's Fort McHenry.

A few miles from the city, General John Stricker and a company of American riflemen surprised Ross. They began to snipe at the British from every direction. Stricker was soon forced to retreat, but not before one of his sharpshooters killed British General Ross. The British soon resumed their march toward Baltimore under the command of Colonel Arthur Brooke, but the brief battle had been costly. The British lost over 300 men, including General Ross. American casualties numbered about 200. Stricker had quickly shown the British that Baltimore was not as unprepared for battle as Washington had been.

On September 13, 1814, the Royal Navy opened fire on Fort McHenry while Brooke began the assault against Baltimore on land. For a day and a night, the British fired mortars, rockets, and shells. The one thousand Americans inside the fort under the command of Major George Armistead did not fire in return. It would have been useless, since the enemy ships were beyond the range of the fort's

You can see the American flag flying over Fort McHenry in this depiction of the British bombardment of the fort.

guns. During the next twenty-five hours, the British fired more than fifteen hundred rounds at the fort. However, damage to the fort was minimal. Only four Americans were killed and twenty-four wounded. The Royal Navy also failed in its attempt to capture Baltimore's waterfront battery and to land troops south of the city.

On shore, British Colonel Brooke tried twice to break through the well-fortified American lines. Each time, his troops were pushed back. Brooke met with Cochrane on September 15, and the two commanders agreed that Baltimore was not worth the effort. The British pulled out later that day.

Francis Scott Key

Francis Scott Key, a prominent Washington lawyer, had watched the siege of Fort McHenry throughout the September night. Key had come to the British fleet to arrange for the release of an American prisoner of war. After he completed his mission, the British refused to put him ashore until the attack on Fort McHenry was over. Key paced the ship all night, watching the bombardment. On the morning of September 14, he was overjoyed to see the American flag still flying, a flag so big it could easily be seen from a ship in the harbor.

Key, a poet, was inspired by the sight. He immediately jotted down the first draft of some verses on the back of a letter he had in his pocket. These were later revised, set to the tune of an old British drinking song, and entitled "The Star-Spangled Banner." The song eventually became the American national anthem.

The Next British Target

The British now set their sights on New Orleans, where produce worth a million dollars sat on the docks. With blessings from Spain, a country allied with Great Britain in its fight to defeat Napoleon in Europe, the British fleet occupied Pensacola, Florida, and planned its attack.

8

PEACE ON CHRISTMAS EVE?

"THERE SHALL BE A FIRM AND UNIVERSAL PEACE BETWEEN HIS BRITANNIC MAJESTY AND THE UNITED STATES, AND BETWEEN THEIR RESPECTIVE COUNTRIES, TERRITORIES, CITIES, TOWNS, AND PEOPLE, OF EVERY DEGREE, WITHOUT EXCEPTION OF PLACES OR PERSONS. ALL HOSTILITIES, BOTH BY SEA AND LAND, SHALL CEASE..."

—Excerpt from the Treaty of Ghent, December 24, 1814

By 1814, the United States' war record had highs and lows. There had been victorious moments on the Great Lakes and on the high seas. The defense of Fort McHenry had been a stunning loss for the British Royal Navy.

American defeats unfortunately offset these victories. Canada had not surrendered and settlers in the Northwest Territory still faced the danger of Indian attacks. The most significant loss however was in Washington. The occupation and burning of public buildings had completely embarrassed the country.

In December 1814, the United States did claim an important triumph in the war, without firing a shot. This battle convened at the negotiating table in Ghent, Belgium. During the peace talks, the American delegation were able to outmaneuver Great Britain. When the treaty was signed on December 24, it was a significant victory, "not because of what the American diplomats won but because of what they avoided losing."[1]

Can War Be Avoided?

The War of 1812 was never popular. Many British, Canadian, and American citizens opposed the war and hoped the two nations would negotiate a treaty quickly. Attempts to end the hostilities began almost as soon as the United States declared war on Great Britain. "The sword was scarcely out of the scabbard," Madison said, "before the enemy was apprised of the reasonable terms on which it would be resheathed."[2]

On June 23, 1812, the President invited Augustus J. Foster, the British minister on assignment in Washington, to the president's mansion and expressed his desire to avoid a serious conflict. The president informed Foster that the British could restore peace at any time by giving up impressment and the Orders in Council. (Though the Orders in Council had been suspended on June 16, 1812, no official agreement had ever been signed by the two countries.)

The British government, preoccupied with the war with Napoleon, also hoped to avoid a confrontation with America. They believed the steps needed to stop the war had already been taken when the Orders in Council were suspended. However, the impressment of sailors was an issue Americans refused to drop, and Foster was informed that the practice must end before negotiations could begin.

Negotiations

In November 1813, President Madison accepted Great Britain's offer to begin peace negotiations. He appointed John Quincy Adams, James Bayard, Henry Clay, Jonathan Russell, and Albert Gallatin to bargain on behalf of the United States.

Now that the war with Napoleon had ended, the English were angry with the United States. They believed that the war in America had aided France. *The London Sun* printed that the American people must not be "left in a condition to repeat their insults, injuries and wrongs."[3]

After agreeing to meet in Ghent, Belgium, Great Britain was in no hurry to sit down and talk. They hoped that victories in America would strengthen their bargaining position.

The American delegates' first instructions were to negotiate the terms of blockades, contraband, and maritime rights of neutral countries during war. They were also told that the treaty must put an end to impressments, and to try to secure

Canada for the United States. The five American delegates quickly realized that these were impossible goals.

When the mood in Great Britain reached Washington in June 1814, Madison and his cabinet decided to drop the issue of impressment. These new instructions did not arrive in time for the first meeting.

First Meetings

It was August before Great Britain's commissioners, Lord James Gambier, a naval officer; Henry Goulburn, a government undersecretary; and Dr. William Adams, a lawyer, arrived in Ghent. All three were inexperienced negotiators who had the authority only to deliver messages between the American delegates and the British government.

The Americans came to the first meeting on August 8, 1814, ready to address the issue of impressment. The British commissioners flatly refused to discuss the issue. Instead, they demanded that "retention of conquered territory" be a starting point for negotiations.[4] The Canadian border was to be adjusted in Canada's favor to include parts of the states of Maine and New York.

American Indians, who had aided the British, were also to be given most of the lands in the old Northwest Territory. The Americans were astounded.[5] When Gallatin asked what should be done with the hundred thousand white settlers who lived in the proposed Indian state, Dr. Adams replied that "They must shift for themselves."[6] Great Britain claimed the right to navigate the Mississippi River, and Americans were to forfeit fishing rights on British shores in the North Atlantic. These demands were unacceptable to the American delegation, and since the British refused to discuss impressment, it appeared that the peace talks' first session would be the last. However, that very evening, the new instructions arrived from Washington.

Clay suspected that Great Britain was trying to gain time, hoping that victories in America would strengthen its bargaining power. He suggested that the delegates wait and see what the British commission's next move would be.

Clay's theory proved right. The British government did not want the negotiations to end. The commissioners soon indicated that they were willing to give in on some issues. At a second meeting, on August 19, Gambier presented a "modified" British proposal. In this plan, the United States would give up the northernmost portion of Maine. Great Britain would control all forts on the Great Lakes and be guaranteed rights to the Mississippi River.

Finally, the British demanded that the border of the Indian state fall along the line set by the Treaty of Greenville, an agreement signed in 1795. The tribes who had signed the treaty lived in the Northwest Territory. This meant that lands now part of the Indiana, Illinois, Wisconsin, and Michigan territories, and the state of Ohio would have to be returned.

The American delegates asked that the British proposals be put in writing, then spent four days working on a reply on which they could all agree. Adams wrote the first draft, then he and the others spent hours revising. Finally, on August 25—the night the British burned Washington—the American delegates signed their response. The note was brief and to the point. It rejected the idea of an Indian state and of British military control over the Great Lakes.

As they sent their reply to the British, the Americans believed that this would end the negotiations. Only Clay still thought the British were bluffing. He was right again. The British were trying to determine what the United States might be willing to give up. They did not want the talks to be abandoned now or England would be blamed for ending the hope of peace. The government prepared new instructions for the British commissioners.

Negotiations Drag On

After a few attempts at insignificant changes and bluffing by both sides, the British government finally told their commissioners to give up the idea of an Indian state. This information was passed on to the American delegation on October 8. The British proposed that the Indians keep the same territories they held in 1811 before the outbreak of war. This item, the first that the two commissions agreed on, was a beginning.

Now each delegation began to prepare its version of a treaty. In the beginning, the Americans were at a disadvantage since the news of the burning of Washington had finally reached Ghent. However, this changed when details of Great Britain's unsuccessful campaign on Baltimore arrived.

The issue of impressment was ignored by both delegations, and the British government soon dropped its demand for military control of the Great Lakes. However, the peace negotiations dragged on as the British delegates raised issue after issue.

New Instructions

By the end of 1814, British treaty negotiations with France were not going smoothly. There was even fear that Napoleon would regain power, and that the fighting in Europe might begin again. Political pressure was directed at the British government to end the war with the United States. The country's citizens demanded relief from the heavy taxes needed to support war—first in Europe and now in America. They encouraged their government not to humiliate the United States at the peace table. Most regretted the destruction of Washington, fearing that that incident alone would encourage the Americans to continue the fight. For these reasons, word was sent to the British commissioners at Ghent to get as good a settlement as possible, but not to push for unreasonable demands. Meanwhile, the United States also faced great difficulties. Trade was at a standstill. The government was out of funds. There were not enough new recruits to replace soldiers in the regular army who had been killed or wounded in battle. Finally, there was a growing movement in the New England states to secede from the rest of the union. New instructions were also sent to the American delegates. They were free to negotiate a peace agreement based on a return to a prewar status. The sticky issues of boundaries and maritime rights of neutral nations could be left for future negotiations.

Christmas Eve Treaty

On December 1, 1814, the two delegations met for the first time since August 19. The Americans now had a significant advantage over the British commissioners. They knew exactly what they wanted to accomplish—peace with no concessions.

During the next several meetings, the Americans became more and more confident. John Quincy Adams and his colleagues drafted a treaty based on the "status quo ante bellum," the status before the war. Nine of the fifteen articles in this draft were amended and accepted as part of the final document.

The Treaty of Ghent stipulated that all conquests of land were to be returned. Both sides were to end hostilities against the Native Americans. The British abandoned the idea of an Indian state. Nothing at all was said about fishing rights, navigation of the Mississippi River, or boundary problems. Nowhere in the treaty was any reference made to impressment or the maritime rights of neutral countries—the issues that had led to war.

The signing ceremony was set for December 24. After a few small errors were corrected with pen and ink, the Treaty of Ghent, also called the Peace of Christmas Eve, was signed. The documents, which simply restored the conditions that existed before the war, were now official and subject to ratification in Washington and London. As John Quincy Adams accepted his copies, he stated his hopes that this would be the last treaty of peace between Great Britain and the United States. Now the American delegates could return home. The war was officially over.

An Official End, Delayed

The British commissioners delivered the documents to their government on December 26, 1814, and the treaty was quickly signed.

Unfortunately, there was no speedy way to deliver the news to Washington or to the British fleet sailing for the American port of New Orleans—it took several weeks to make the

On December 24, 1814, the Treaty of Ghent—also called the Peace of Christmas Eve—was signed.

journey from Britain to America by sea. On January 2, 1815, as Henry Carroll, Clay's personal secretary, and Anthony Baker, a representative of the British government, sailed for America with a copy of the treaty, preparations for the final confrontation of the War of 1812 were under way. Delayed by bad weather, their ship did not dock in New York City until February 11.

After landing, Carroll let officials know he carried the signed Treaty of Ghent. Leaflets were printed to announce the war had ended. Soon the city was celebrating. Schools were closed. People left their jobs. Church bells rang. Troops fired guns to salute the good news. One rider carried the report to Boston. He made the trip in thirty-two hours, spreading the news across the region in record time. Official copies of the treaty arrived in Washington on February 14, ten days after news of General Andrew Jackson's victory at the Battle of New Orleans.

On February 16, the United States Senate voted unanimously to ratify the Treaty of Ghent, and President Madison signed the document later that day. The war officially came to an end at 11:00 p.m. on February 17, 1815.

By the time this news reached England, Napoleon had reclaimed power in France, and the British government had learned of the disaster at New Orleans. Great Britain was relieved that the United States had ratified the treaty so quickly.[7]

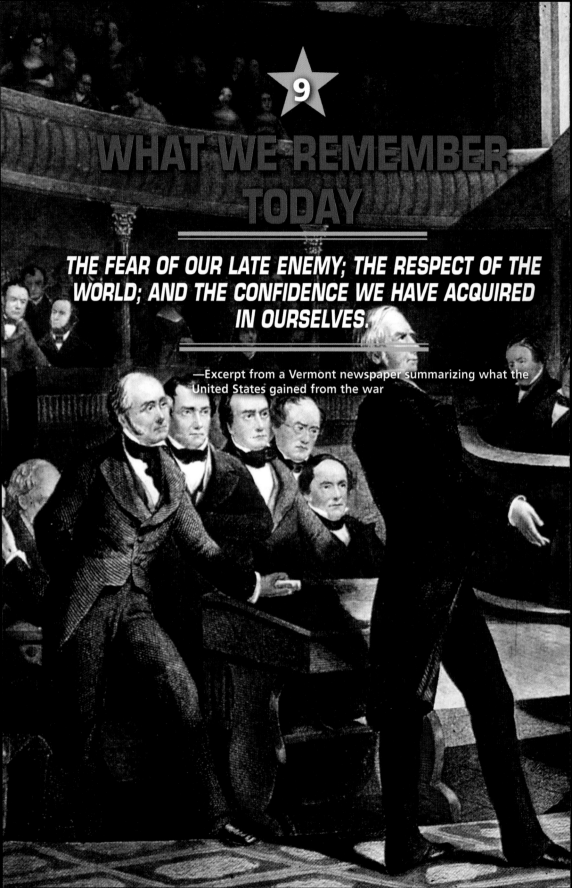

★9

WHAT WE REMEMBER TODAY

THE FEAR OF OUR LATE ENEMY; THE RESPECT OF THE WORLD; AND THE CONFIDENCE WE HAVE ACQUIRED IN OURSELVES.

—Excerpt from a Vermont newspaper summarizing what the United States gained from the war

At the end of the War of 1812, Americans were quick to forget their losses. Citizens looked to the future with a new-found confidence. Feelings of political unity grew. Gallatin, one of the delegates at Ghent, wrote: "The war has renewed and rein-stated the national feelings and character which the Revolution had given, and which were daily lessening. The people now...are more American; they feel and act more as a nation; I hope that the permanency of the Union is there-by better served."[1]

The war also strengthened America's founding principles. The republican government—a government by the people, for the people— was something new, an experiment. The young country had proved it could deal with a crisis successfully while working within the limits of its constitution. In that sense, the War of 1812 could be considered America's second war of independence.

In both conflicts, either as English colonists or as citizens of the United States, the population objected to being forced to obey Great Britain's dictates. However, in 1812, it was the country's national pride that was threatened rather than any real attempt on Great Britain's part to reclaim the United States as a colony.

The communication and transportation of the day influenced events that led to the War of 1812. In fact, conflict might have been avoided completely if sailing ships had not been the speediest way to deliver news across the Atlantic Ocean. However, this strange little war, the United States' second and last struggle against Great Britain, and the second and last time it tried to conquer Canada, was a turning point in American history.

Battle Experience

A look back to 1812 shows clearly how unprepared the United States was to fight a war. The fact that the country did not lose its independence or at least a portion of its territory was miraculous. In the end, it was more luck than military expertise that prevented the map of the United States from being redrawn in Canada's favor.

America's Army and Navy won few victories during the two years and eight months of the War of 1812 because the country was so unprepared. Beginning in 1801, the Republican-controlled Congress cut defense spending. The regular army was reduced to 3,300 men. This small force had little training and even less battle experience. Construction on new navy ships was stopped, and most of the frigates were removed from service.

Leadership, civil and military, was also ineffective. The old and feeble military generals recruited during the War of 1812 were poor leaders and tactical planners. Younger officers lacked experience and were often unable to control the men under their command. Endless debates in Congress delayed or prevented the adoption of laws needed to raise an army and create taxes to pay for the war effort. James Madison, who was a weak, indecisive president, was unable to push necessary legislation through Congress. He was also slow to remove incompetent generals in the field and ineffective members of his own cabinet, or to promote officers who had proven themselves in battle. Because of these problems, permanent changes were made after the war. The *Niles Weekly Register* printed in May 1815 stated, "the best way to avoid war is probably to be prepared to meet it with firmness and effect."[2] The United States created a larger standing navy and army. Aides with battle experience were assigned to key positions to train recruits. America's commitment to a strong military forced Europe to take her more seriously.

Another important outcome of the war was Great Britain's new attitude. They began to recognize "that the friendship of the United States was a major asset..."[3]

The two enemies entered a new relationship, a peaceful one that has stood the test of time. Today, Britian and the United States are allies, rather than enemies.

Winning the Peace Talks

In the peace negotiations at Ghent, Belgium, however, the United States' record was much better. At the table the American delegates consistently outmaneuvered the British and achieved a victory because of what they avoided losing.

John Quincy Adams and his associates took a firm stand from the beginning. They flatly refused to discuss the first British demands made on August 8, 1814: the "retention of conquered territory," the return of lands in the old Northwest to the American Indians, and the right to navigate the Mississippi River.[4]

In the final negotiated version, the British gave up on all these issues. The Treaty of Ghent ordered all conquered lands returned. The idea of an Indian state was abandoned, and nothing at all was said about Mississippi River navigation rights. As for the issues that had led to war, impressment and maritime right of neutral countries, they were also completely ignored.

Though the American delegates had managed to do exactly what they had been instructed to do—negotiate a return to the way things had been before the war—they were nervous about the treaty's reception in the United States, since they had not gained any real ground.[5] However, Americans viewed the Battle of New Orleans as a victorious end to the war, and nobody paid much attention to the details of the peace treaty now that the war was over.[5] The public saw survival as a victory.

Gains and Losses

American manufacturing benefited from the embargo, non-intercourse, and the war itself. War increased the demand for manufactured products, but also made it impossible to import enough goods. The United States, in fact, was cut off from Great Britain, its main supplier of factory-made products. The result was an industrial explosion in the United States that, in a time of peace, would probably have taken twenty years.

The War of 1812 was also a victory for those who supported territorial expansion. Despite Native American protests, America set its sights on the West and never looked back. The Northwest Territory was soon settled by Americans and then carved up into the new states of Indiana, Illinois, Michigan and Wisconsin.

Ultimately, this means that, sadly, the real losers in the War of 1812 were the American Indians. Tecumseh's confederacy was the last serious attempt to unite the native nations to resist the white settlers overrunning their hunting grounds. In the summer of 1815, the United States signed treaties with the fifteen tribes who had fought alongside the British. In these treaties, the American Indians were promised all the territories they controlled in 1811. However, these agreements were basically ignored. In the end, not one acre of land was ever returned to the Native Americans.

In addition to not giving up these Indian lands, the United States also retained control of part of the Spanish territory of West Florida that had been seized in 1813 as part of Jackson's preparations to protect the Gulf coast of the United States from British invasion. The stage was set for a period of westward expansion that would finally end when the fiftieth state, Hawaii, joined the union in 1959.

Names Recorded for History

Francis Scott Key, inspired by patriotism when he saw Fort McHenry's American flag still flying after the British siege, penned a poem. He is best remembered today as the author of the American national anthem, "The Star-Spangled Banner." Key died in 1843, but his final resting place was not determined until 1898. Today his remains are buried at Mount Olivet Cemetery in Frederick, Maryland. A sculpture of the poet tops a granite monument. Key appears to be waving his hat with joy as he spots the banner still flying over Fort McHenry. The American flag now flies over Key's grave twenty-four hours a day, seven days a week.

Francis Scott Key is shown pointing and celebrating that the "flag was still there."

Many others, recognized as American heroes during the war, were later elected to important government positions. John Quincy Adams served as secretary of state under President James Monroe. In 1824, John Quincy Adams, following in his father's footsteps became the sixth president of the United States.

Henry Clay continued as the Speaker of the House of Representatives after the war, and was elected to the Senate in 1831. Clay and General Andrew Jackson faced off in the presidential election of

Dolley Madison was known for her social graces and threw many parties and gatherings while her husband was in office.

1832. Jackson won and completed two terms.

William Henry Harrison entered Congress in 1816 and later became a senator. In 1840, he defeated Henry Clay for the presidency. Harrison's military record and his slogan "Tippecanoe and Tyler, too" won him a landslide victory. One month after his inauguration, Harrison died of pneumonia. His vice president, John Tyler, took over and became the tenth president of the United States.

Even First Lady Dolley Madison earned a place in history for her coolheadedness during battle. Years later, she wrote to a newspaper explaining why she ordered the servants to save the portrait: "I acted thus because of my respect for General Washington, not that I felt a desire to gain laurels; but, should there be a merit in remaining an hour in danger of life and liberty to save the likeness of anything, the merit in this case belongs to me."[6] The story of Dolley's determined efforts to save a piece of American history, George

Washington's portrait, makes her one of the
United States' most famous First Ladies.

A Walk Back in Time

The War of 1812 has sometimes been called the
forgotten war. However, even today visitors can
step back through time and visit places where
many of the important events took place.

In Battle Ground, Indiana, a museum sits near
the Tippecanoe Battlefield, where William Henry
Harrison defeated the Shawnee warriors led by
The Prophet. The site of the Raisin River Massacre
is preserved near Monroe, Michigan. Visitors can
also walk the battlefield where Andrew Jackson
defeated the British and learn more about the
famous pirate and privateer Jean Lafitte at the
Chalmette National Historical Park in New Orleans,
Louisiana.

The Sackets Harbor Battlefield and Navy Yard
Restoration State Historic Site in New York State
features two museums. Displays inside the
Commandant's House and in the 1812 Navy Exhibit
tell about the history of the town and its part in
the war. Oliver Hazard Perry's flagship, the USS
Niagara, can be seen in Erie, Pennsylvania, and a
memorial to his victory on Lake Erie stands in Put-
in-Bay, Ohio (near Sandusky).

In May 2015, The USS *Constitution,* fondly
remembered as "Old Ironsides," was moved from
Boston Harbor to the Charlestown Navy Yard's Dry
Dock One for restoration. The navy constructed a

"Old Ironsides" sits in drydock as repairs are made.

viewing stand for visitors to watch as the old vessel was raised from the water. By June 8, the ship was secured and stable. Once again visitors were invited aboard the "Old Ironsides." They can walk the decks, even while work goes on, with marines dressed in naval uniforms of the early 1800s, and listen to tales of the ship's colorful past.

In Perrysburg, Ohio, Fort Meigs has been reconstructed on its original site. Exhibits about the history of the area and its role in the War of 1812 are displayed in seven blockhouses on the fort grounds. Our country's flag still waves twenty-four hours a day over Baltimore's Fort McHenry. The star-shaped fort has been restored and is open to visitors.

Fort McHenry's Huge Banner

The star-spangled banner that Key saw on the morning of September 14, 1814, is now on display at the Smithsonian Institute in Washington, D.C. It was gifted to the Institute in 1912. The flag turned over to the Smithsonian was 8 feet (2.4 m) shorter than the one sewn by Mary Pickersgill. More than 200 yards (183 m) of fabric were missing including one star.

In 1998, the star-spangled banner was taken off display for restoration. After a thorough examination, conservators decided to remove a linen lining added in 1914. The lining forced the flag into a uniform rectangle, instead of its true, irregular shape. Working with scissors and tweezers, 1.7 million stitches were tediously removed. A moveable bridge suspended above the flag allowed workers to reach middle sections and not damage the original fabric.

When the lining was finally removed, everyone was amazed. The colors under the linen, protected from light and dirt, were still bright. The restoration project took eight years. The price tag was 8.5 million dollars. And even after all that time and money, the flag was still not ready for display.

Mary's flag was far too fragile to hang vertically again. A special display area needed to be created. In 2006, a $19 million chamber was designed and built. It would protect the banner from light, air, and water. The flag rested on a

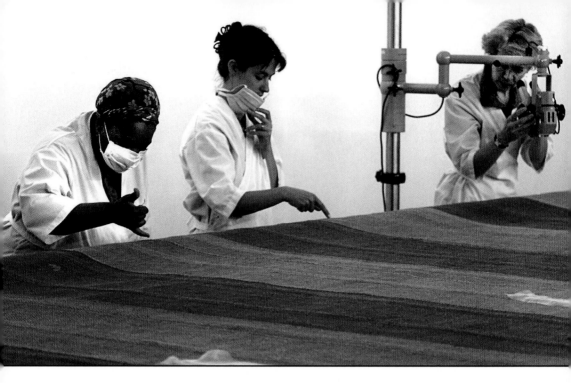

These women are working on restoring the "Star-Spangled Banner".

platform, tilted at a ten-degree angle for viewing. In November 2008, the star-spangled banner exhibit reopened to the public. The effect was inspiring.

The banner seemed to float in the dimly lit room. Though tattered and frail, its colors are brilliant and alive. The holes and tears from use over the years are plainly visible, a testament to all those who lost their lives during the War of 1812. Two hundred years after the battle the star-spangled banner still proudly waves for all to see.

Who Really Won?

One author called this conflict "the war nobody won."[7] However, having won the last battle, the Americans were convinced that they won the War of 1812. The Canadians, having stopped the

American invasion, believed that they had won the war. And the British, having given up nothing that they considered important, were also convinced that they had won.

Perhaps the phrase that best describes this time in the history of the United States is "the incredible War of 1812."[8] From beginning to end, with all its twists and turns, this early chapter in American history is full of interesting events and characters that helped make the United States what it is today.

Chronology

1806—Great Britain proclaims a blockade of the European coast; Napoleon blockades the British Isles.

1807—Jefferson recommends and Congress passes the Embargo Act of 1807; British Royal Navy fires on the USS Chesapeake on June 22.

1809—James Madison inaugurated on March 4; Embargo Act is repealed and replaced by the Non-Intercourse Act in March.

1811—The Prophet defeated by William Henry Harrison on November 7 at Battle of Tippecanoe.

1812—Madison signs War Bill on June 18; Great Britain captures Fort Michilimackinac on July 17; Fort Dearborn massacre on August 15; General Henry Dearborn surrenders to the British at Detroit on August 16; Battle of Queenston fought on October 13; United States Army retreats from eastern Canada by November 23.

1813—Battle of Frenchtown on January 22; Raisin River Massacre on January 23; Battle of York fought on April 27; Battle of Fort George on May 27; Battle of Sackets Harbor on May 29; Battle of Lake Erie on September 10; Battle of the Thames on October 5; Great Britain offers to begin peace negotiations with the United States on November 4; United States adopts embargo on December 17.

1814—Napoleon relinquishes the throne on April 11; United States repeals the Embargo Act; Peace negotiations begin in Ghent on August 8; Battle of Bladensburg on August 25; British burn Washington on August 24–25; Battle of Baltimore fought on September 13–14; Francis Scott Key writes the "Star-Spangled Banner" on September 14; Battle of Lake Borgne on December 14;

skirmishes around New Orleans from December 23–January 15, 1815; United States and Great Britain sign the Treaty of Ghent on December 24.

1815—Battle of New Orleans on January 8; Treaty of Ghent reaches the United States on February 11; United States Senate approves the treaty on February 16 and Madison signs; United States and Great Britain exchange ratifications ending the War of 1812 on February 17.

1898—Francis Scott Key's remains buried at Mount Olivet Cemetery in Frederick, Maryland.

1998–2008—Smithsonian restoration project for Mary Pickersgill's star-spangled banner.

2012—War of 1812 Bicentennial.

2015—In May, the USS *Constitution* moved to the Charlestown Navy Yard's Dry Dock One for restoration. It is expected to take about three years to complete the project.

Chapter Notes

FOREWORD

1. Peter Snow, *When Britain Burned the White House: The 1814 Invasion of Washington* (New York: Thomas Dunne Books, 2014), p. 188.

CHAPTER 1.   "ALMOST INCREDIBLE VICTORY!"

1. Samuel Carter III, *Blaze of Glory: the Fight for New Orleans, 1814-1815* (New York: St. Martin's Press, 1971), p. 104.
2. Ibid.
3. Ibid.
4. Albert Marrin, *1812: The War Nobody Won* (New York: Atheneum, 1985), p. 151.
5. Hugh Howard, *Mr. and Mrs. Madison's War: America's First Couple and the Second War of Independence* (New York: Bloomsbury Press, 2012), p. 264.
6. Ibid., 265.
7. Donald R. Hickey, The War of 1812: A Forgotten Conflict (Urbana: University of Illinois Press, 1989), p. 209.
8. Howard, p. 270.
9. Ibid., p. 271.
10. Hickey, p. 212.
11. Ibid.
12. Ibid.
13. Howard, p. 270.

CHAPTER 2.   MR. MADISON'S WAR

1. Hugh Howard, *Mr. and Mrs. Madison's War: America's First Couple and the Second War of Independence*, (New York: Bloomsbury Press, 2012), pp. 1–2.
2. Ibid., p. 2.
3. Harry L. Coles, *The War of 1812* (Chicago: University of Chicago Press, 1965), p. 4.
4. Ibid., p. 7.
5. Donald R. Hickey, *The War of 1812: A Forgotten Conflict* (Urbana: University of Illinois Press, 1989), p. 25.
6. Jeremy Black, *The War of 1812 in the Age of Napoleon* (Norman: University of Oklahoma Press, 2009), p. 42.
7. Ibid., p. 37.
8. Howard, p. 25.

CHAPTER 3. DEFENDING UPPER CANADA

1. Alan Taylor, *The Civil War of 1812, American Citizens, British Subjects, Irish Rebels, & Indian Allies* (New York: Alfred A. Knopf, 2010), p. 149.
2. A. J. Langguth, *Union 1812: The Americans Who Fought the Second War of Independence* (New York: Simon & Schuster, 2006), p. 187.
3. Ibid., 188.
4. Harry L. Coles, *The War of 1812* (Chicago: University of Chicago Press, 1965), p. 52.
5. Taylor, p.155.
6. Pierre Berton, *The Invasion of Canada 1812–1813* (Toronto: McClelland and Steward, 1980), p. 123.
7. Coles, p. 53.
8. Donald R. Hickey, *The War of 1812: A Forgotten Conflict* (Urbana: University of Illinois Press, 1989), p. 84.
9. Berton, p. 99.

CHAPTER 4. AMERICA'S NAVY TAKES THE SEAS

1. Hugh Howard, *Mr. and Mrs. Madison's War: America's First Couple and the Second War of Independence* (New York: Bloomsbury Press, 2012), p. 49.
2. Ibid.
3. Ibid.
4. Ibid., p. 50.
5. Ibid.
6. Harry L. Coles, *The War of 1812* (Chicago: University of Chicago Press, 1965), p. 80.
7. Donald R. Hickey, *The War of 1812: A Forgotten Conflict* (Urbana: University of Illinois Press, 1989), p. 94.
8. Ibid.
9. Coles, p. 87.
10. Hickey, p. 96.
11. John K. Mahon, *The War of 1812* (Gainesville: The University of Florida Press, 1972), p. 123.
12. Ibid., pp. 124–125.
13. George C. Daughan, *1812: The Navy's War* (New York: Basic Books, 2011), p. 149.

CHAPTER 5. FIGHT FOR THE FRONTIER

1. George C. Daughan, *1812: The Navy's War* (New York: Basic Books, 2011), p. 101.

2. Ibid.

3. Harry L. Coles, *The War of 1812* (Chicago: University of Chicago Press, 1965), p. 113.

4. A. J. Langguth, *Union 1812: The Americans Who Fought the Second War of Independence* (New York: Simon & Schuster, 2006), p. 240.

5. Ibid.

6. Coles., p. 119.

7. Ibid., p. 121.

8. Daughan, p. 217.

9. Donald R. Hickey, *The War of 1812: A Forgotten Conflict* (Urbana: University of Illinois Press, 1989), p. 137.

10. Langguth, p. 270.

CHAPTER 6. COMMODORE OLIVER HAZARD PERRY

1. Harry L. Coles, *The War of 1812* (Chicago: University of Chicago Press, 1965), p. 108.

2. George C. Daughan, *1812: The Navy's War* (New York: Basic Books, 2011), p. 177.

3. Donald R. Hickey, *The War of 1812: A Forgotten Conflict* (Urbana: University of Illinois Press, 1989), p. 130.

4. A. J. Langguth, *Union 1812: The Americans Who Fought the Second War of Independence* (New York: Simon & Schuster, 2006), p. 248.

5. Coles, p. 124.

6. Hickey, p. 314.

7. Ibid., p. 315.

8. Coles, p. 129.

CHAPTER 7. WASHINGTON UP IN FLAMES

1. Peter Snow, *When Britain Burned the White House: The 1814 Invasion of Washington* (New York: Thomas Dunne Books, 2014), p. 7.

2. Pierre Berton, *Flames Across the Border* (Boston: Little, Brown and Company, 1981), p. 367.

3. Snow, p. 28.

4. A. J. Langguth, *Union 1812: The Americans Who Fought the Second War of Independence* (New York: Simon & Schuster, 2006), p. 298.

5. Berton, p. 366.

6. Snow, p. 63.

7. Ibid., p. 107.

8. Kate Caffrey, *The Twilight's Last Gleaming: British vs. American 1812-1915* (New York: Stein and Day, 1977), p. 238.

9. Ibid.

10. Ibid., p. 239.

11. Ibid., p. 247.

12. Snow, p. 188.

CHAPTER 8.   PEACE ON CHRISTMAS EVE?

1. Donald R. Hickey, *The War of 1812: A Short History* (Urbana: University of Illinois Press, 2012), p. 103.

2. Ibid., p. 104.

3. Donald R. Hickey, *The War of 1812: A Forgotten Conflict* (Urbana: University of Illinois Press, 1989), p. 287.

4. Pierre Berton, *Flames Across the Border* (Boston: Little, Brown and Company, 1981), p. 407.

5. Ibid.

6. John K. Mahon, *The War of 1812* (Gainesville: The University of Florida Press, 1972), p. 381.

7. Ibid.

CHAPTER 9.   WHAT WE REMEMBER TODAY

1. Troy Bickham, *The Weight of Vengeance: The United States, the British Empire, and the War of 1812* (Oxford: University Press, 2012), p. 278.

2. Ibid.

3. George C. Daughan, *1812: The Navy's War* (New York: Basic Books, 2011), p. 414.

4. J. Mackey Hitsman, *The Incredible War of 1812* (Toronto: University of Toronto Press, 1965), p. 232.

5. Pierre Berton, *Flames Across the Border* (Boston: Little, Brown and Company, 1981), p. 424.

6. Steve Vogel, *Through the Perilous Fight*: *Six Weeks That Saved the Nation* (New York: Random House, 2013), p. 402.

7. Albert Marrin, *1812: The War Nobody Won* (New York: Atheneum, 1985), title page.

8. Hitsman, title page.

Glossary

battery—Group of one or more pieces of artillery on a warship or on land for defense.

blockade—Isolation of a nation or area by enemy ships to prevent entrance and exit of traffic and commerce.

bounty—Bonus paid to encourage new recruits to join the militia.

breastworks—A temporary fortification for defense, usually about chest high.

broadside—All guns on one side of a warship.

contraband—Illegal or unacceptable goods that could be seized from enemy ships during wartime.

degradation—To be made lower in quality; made inferior or less valuable.

embargo—A government order prohibiting the movement of merchant ships into and out of ports.

flotilla—A group of small armed boats.

frigate—A fast naval sailing vessel heavily armed on one or two decks.

grape—A cluster of small iron balls, often contained in a canvas bag, that scatter when fired from a cannon.

gun port—An opening in the ship through which cannon muzzles are positioned for firing.

kedging—To move by setting light anchors out in front of the ship, then reeling the ship toward anchors.

impressment—The act of seizing persons and compelling them to serve in the naval forces.

ships of line—A type of warship using a special naval tactic called the line of battle. Two lines of opposing warships would maneuver to bring the greatest broadside firepower to strike the enemy ships.

stockade—A defensive enclosure, like a fort, constructed from stakes and timbers driven upright into the ground one beside the other.

touch hole—The opening in early cannons where the charge was lighted.

For More Information

Books

Clarke, Gordon. *Major Battles of the War of 1812.* New York: Crabtree Publishing Company, 2012.

Crump, Jennifer. *Canada on Fire: The War of 1812.* Toronto: Dundurn Press, 2011.

Dale, Ronald. *The Invasion of Canada: Battles of the War of 1812.* Toronto: James Lorimer & Company Ltd., 2012.

MacDonald, Cheryl. *Isaac Brock: Canada's Hero of the War of 1812.* Toronto: James Lorimer & Company Ltd., 2012.

Olsen, Eric. *Tecumseh: Nature's Patriot.* New York: Henry Holt, 2012.

Websites

Fort McHenry, National Monument and Historic Shrine
www.nps.gov/fomc/index.htm
History and facts about Fort McHenry and the Star-Spangled Banner.

Smithsonian Institution, the Star-Spangled Banner
amhistory.si.edu/starspangledbanner/making-the-flag.aspx
The history behind the making of the star-spangled banner.

USS *Constitution*: Restoring the Legend.
www.navy.mil/ah_online/constitution/index.html
Information on the USS Constitution *and its restoration.*

Index